P9-BYB-444

About the Author

Cassandra Eason is an international author, broadcaster and psychic consultant. She has studied the history, psychology and esoteric practices of the Tarot for a number of years and has read the Tarot on numerous radio and television programmes thoughout the world as well as lecturing on and teaching the subject to a variety of audiences. She has written 18 books on the paranormal, magic and divination, spiritual and religious experiences and is an expert on folklore and superstition.

Psychic Awareness

Piatkus Guides

Other titles in this series include

Celtic Wisdom
Crystal Wisdom
The Essential Nostradamus
Feng Shui
Meditation
Reiki
Tarot

A PIATKUS GUIDE

Psychic Awareness

Cassandra Eason

PIATKUS

Visit the Piatkus website!

Piatkus publishes a wide range of exciting fiction and non-fiction, including books on health, mind body & spirit, sex, self-help, cookery, biography and the paranormal.

If you want to:
- read descriptions of our popular titles
- buy our books over the internet
- take advantage of our special offers
- enter our monthly competition
- learn more about your favourite Piatkus authors

visit our website at:

www.piatkus.co.uk

© 1999 Cassandra Eason

First published in 1999 by
Judy Piatkus (Publishers) Ltd
5 Windmill Street, London W1T 2JA
e-mail: info@piatkus.co.uk

Reprinted 2001

The moral rights of the author have been asserted

A catalogue record for this book is available from the British Library

ISBN 0-7499-1932-9

Designed by Sue Ryall

Set in 12.5/14 pt Perpetua
Typeset by Action Publishing Technology Limited, Gloucester
Printed & bound in Great Britain by
Mackays of Chatham PLC

Contents

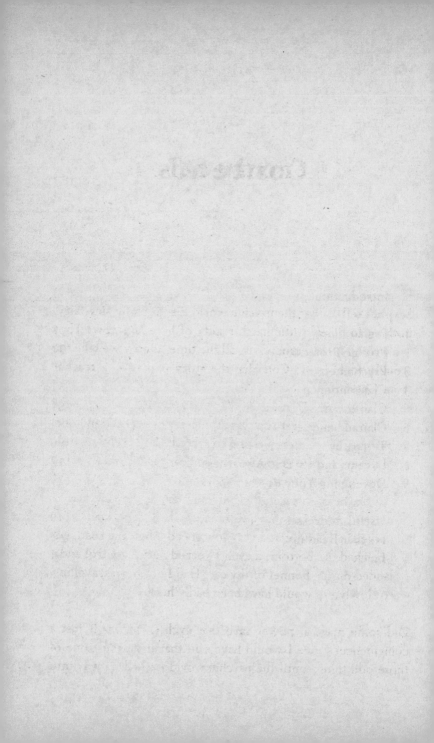

Introduction

Sceptics tell us that the psychic world is something airy-fairy, nothing to do with the harsh reality of here and now. They are wrong. It is all around us, all the time, if only we take the trouble to heed it. Consider the story of Paula, a teacher from Cheshire:

> When my youngest son was at nursery he warned me one morning as we were driving to school: 'Be careful, Mummy, we are going to bang the car on the nursery road.'
> I drove extra carefully to the nursery as the lane was narrow. After I dropped my son at school, I was still nervous and drove at a very low speed down the road. As I reached the bottom, a cyclist veered out of control and landed on the bonnet of my car. Had I not been travelling so slowly, he would have been badly hurt.

Did some magical power save that cyclist, or was it just a coincidence? Once I would have said that it was just one of those odd things until the psychic world pushed its way into my own life. One morning my son Jack, then aged two and a half, casually told me that his father had fallen off his motorbike but was unhurt. Unknown to me, at that very moment my husband John was having a motorbike accident 40 miles away, although he was, as Jack had reported, unhurt.

After this incident I began exploring the psychic world of ordinary children. I found that many people, adults as well as children, demonstrated a strong intuitive sense. Not only could they predict danger for their loved ones, but they were also able to read each other's minds, sense ghosts and pick up impressions of the past from inanimate objects.

These innate intuitive abilities are the same power that prompts a mother to wake in the night routinely before an infant, or an adult to phone his or her own mother at an unusual time or in a moment of stress to find the number engaged; the mother is dialling them at precisely that moment. Such psychic links, prompted by love, occur between siblings, grandparents and grandchildren, partners and even friends. It is these instincts that lie behind psychic awareness. As I have researched the subject over the last ten years and published 20 books on all aspects of these amazing powers, I have become increasingly aware that these paranormal powers can be effectively developed by everyone.

What is Psychic Awareness?

Psychic awareness begins in and is transmitted through our five physical senses. With practice, these can be extended past the normal range of, for example, sight to give second sight and to such areas as telepathy (mind-to-mind communication), clairaudience (hearing what is not physically present), clairsentience (sensing what is not accessible by normal channels), clairvoyance (seeing both places and people far off, especially in other dimensions) and psychometry (gaining information by touch). The psyche or soul that has access to thousands of years of wisdom is the source of out-of-body travelling, and creative dreamwork is accessed through the imagination.

As our psychic senses develop, they not only operate more efficiently as an early warning system, but can be used in divination and dream interpretation so that decision-making can be based, not merely on information accessible to the conscious minds, but the deep unconscious wisdom just out of reach by conventional thought processes.

In teaching as well as developing my own psychic awareness, I have discovered that we all have our unique paths. The most useful suggestions I have made to students and in books I have written are those that have triggered methods of exploration that might be totally different from mine, but which work for the person concerned. Using the feedback from both students in my classes, from radio and TV phone-ins and from letters from readers, I have modified my original ideas, and continue to do so.

The psychic world is fluid and constantly evolving. With each new stage of life and the rapidly changing world in which we live, the methods and interpretations inevitably and rightly evolve.

How to Use this Book

I begin with ways of accessing your psychic wisdom through such skills as meditation and visualisation, as well as psychic protection. If you are new to psychic exploration, it is worth spending a little time exploring these concepts, as they make learning specific skills easier. If you are more experienced, you may wish to start with a specific area that interests you, and perhaps experiment with alternative ways of using your existing ability. The topics are all inter-related and interchangeable.

Psychometry – gaining intuitive impressions through touch – is a good entry point to the different skills for beginners, as you may find that the other intuitive arts, such as clairvoyance and clairsentience, are naturally triggered through physical contact with old objects or ancient sites.

You can work either alone or with friends and in time give readings for people you do not know well. Each chapter contains an optional exercise, and these and other suggested activities throughout the book can form the focus for an informal psychic evening with friends.

Outings with friends or family members to stately homes, standing stones or ruined abbeys may detect ghostly presences or tune into the energies of the past. Above all, the book is a chance to return the psychic to where it belongs, in our hearts and our homes, so that it incorporates laughter and fun and is not a mysterious art that is divorced from reality and common sense.

A decade ago I was a total sceptic, with a degree in psychology and ten years' teaching experience behind me. Now I have learned that there is a place for logic, for traditional learning and for healthy scepticism, but there are also times when it is important to gaze into a candle flame or to close my eyes and let the intuitive wisdom flow and the inner voice speak true. In spite of all our tests, we will never precisely know how a young child can tune into his father hitting the tarmac 40 miles away or how a dream or symbol seen on the surface of a mirror or in moonlit water can offer accurate insights into unformulated questions and offer guidance to the best future path.

Keeping a Psychic Journal

If you keep a notebook or ring binder of your psychic explor-ations, you can record the results of your work, create or adapt your own symbol system and make notes of special dreams and readings you do for others. As well as marking your progress, you can use this journal to collect paranormal family experiences, such as children's invisible friends, examples of a child reading a mother's mind, a man or woman's telepathic links with a partner, moments of positive precognition, dates when you sensed a deceased grandma's perfume. We always think we will remember these precious examples of love and wonder, but it is very easy to forget details over the years.

Also you may like to record incidents of colourful family history, remedies, tales of a great grandfather who walked 50 miles from the countryside to the city or Romany family links. These legends are the folklore of tomorrow; if we cease to tell stories of family myth and wisdom to our children, so our personal spiritual culture is lost.

You can copy the most precious of these memories into a special leather-bound book, where you can also collect photographs of ancient sites you have visited, facts and legends about the ghosts you may have seen or sensed, pressed flowers and herbs collected from special journeys, drawings or paintings inspired by pictures you saw in the clouds or in a candle flame. As I have said many times, we are all magical and special. These insights into the world of the spirit are very precious and part of the legacy we leave for our children. The skills in this book can form the basis for much wider experiments and exploration. If you can read images in ink on water or light reflected on a mirror, you can transfer the skill to reading tea leaves or a crystal ball or to one of the more formal methods of divination, such as runes or Tarot cards.

The Useful Addresses and Further Reading sections at the end of the book provide extra information on how you can develop your psychic awareness in different ways.

EXERCISE: MAKING A MAGICAL TREASURE BOX

We all had treasure boxes as children, filled with shells and stones we found on holiday, special pieces of jewellery, pearl buttons, sequins, lucky charms and perhaps brilliantly coloured feathers.

As you work through this book, you will find that you need a few very simple items: herbs, candles, some essential oil, a quartz crystal, perhaps a crystal pendulum. Because the powers are within us, not the artefacts, you can easily improvise, using a key on a chain for a pendulum, or an ordinary household candle and make-up glass for your candle and mirror pictures.

A treasure box can be a square or oval container of wood or some other natural substance such as raffia, metal or even a strong gold or silver cardboard box. If you can adapt or buy a box that is endowed with joyous or loving memories, the positive emotions will spill over into your psychic work. Items might include:

☆ Small jars or pouches of dried herbs, especially those associated with divination – parsley, sage, rosemary and thyme; and those for harmony and peaceful sleep – dried chamomile flowers and lavender.

☆ Candles of different colours, especially red, gold, silver, white and green and, if possible, an undyed yellow beeswax candle that can be used in any kind of ritual.

☆ A small selection of essential oils: jasmine for the intuition of the Moon, frankincense for the joy of the Sun, patchouli for the communicative powers of Mercury, geranium for the empathy of Venus, peppermint for the impetus to act of Mars, bergamot (which should be kept out of direct sunlight) for the wisdom of Jupiter and tea tree oil for the necessary changes instigated by Saturn.

☆ Lavender and rose are all-purpose healing oils and encourage gentle intuitive wisdom.

☆ A small burner and incense sticks or cones: pine for energy and money, rose for love and healing and sandalwood for both psychic insight and protection.

☆ An uncut and unpolished piece of amethyst or rose quartz large enough to use as a focus and for cleansing other crystals.

☆ A crystal pendulum or a pointed clear crystal quartz.

☆ A small oval mirror for scrying.

☆ Dark silk scarves for wrapping crystals and psychic tools when not in use.

1

Preparation

Psychic awareness begins by recognising those natural intuitive powers that emerge quite spontaneously in everyday life. There are many ways of increasing their effectiveness, so that they not only operate more efficiently in times of need but can be consciously harnessed to give us the power to explore options, rehearse future paths and become more in tune with the hidden as well as expressed feelings and intentions of others.

The First Step: Relaxation

Nothing is more guaranteed to evoke tension than being told to relax. Effective relaxation begins by deliberately tensing your body, part by part, then releasing the tension gradually, so that the physical body and conscious mind quieten and allow the psyche to gain expression.

In this relaxed state you become more receptive to unconscious wisdom, just as dreams and daytime visions can offer solutions and provide inspiration that eludes conscious thought. Five minutes' relaxation before psychic work will naturally open channels of deeper awareness and extend the normal senses so that the sixth sense can begin to operate:

☆ Sit cross-legged on the floor, if this is a naturally comfortable position, or in a chair that supports your back and arms well so that your feet rest gently on the floor. Alternatively you can lie on a bed or bank of cushions with your head and arms supported by pillows.

☆ Starting at your toes, press your right foot against the floor or bed.

☆ Curl your toes into a tight ball and then relax them, visualising them resting on a soft cloud.

☆ Press the left foot against the floor, again tightening the toes and relaxing gradually.

☆ Clench your lower legs as though you were going to kick out. Begin by tensing the right calf, then relaxing it.

☆ Do this with the left and let go, so that each leg is resting against an unseen bank of thistledown.

☆ Tense your thighs, pressing them together, and then relax, once again right followed by left. Then do the same with your buttocks, lower back, stomach, arms, right and left.

☆ Clench your hands simultaneously to make a fist, and then let them fall to your sides, palms uppermost if you are lying down, or resting on the arms of a chair.

☆ Extend your upper spine and neck, letting them gently fall back on to cushions or the bed.

☆ Screw up your eyes, and then relax them.

☆ Finally press your head upwards, as though against a hard car roof, and let it descend.

☆ Listen to your breathing. Gradually and quite naturally let the breaths become deeper and slower.

Visualising Relaxation

Adding imagery to the relaxation process can overcome conscious blocks. Relax your body physically, while visualising your limbs pressing against smooth surfaces or brushed lightly by flowers or butterflies. You can create your own relaxation scenarios, perhaps using a tape of the sea or the wind through a forest (music suppliers are listed at the back of the book).

☆ Feel your feet on warm soft sand. Bury them as deeply as you can, pushing downwards and then releasing your toes to rest once more on the soft, smooth, sunny shore.

☆ See yourself next enclosed in a rainbow bubble. Push upwards with your arms as high as they will go, so that they press but do not penetrate the shimmering upper membrane, and then sink back.

☆ Push outwards now to touch the bubble on either side of you, so that again you feel the pliable indentation, and then return your hands gently to your sides.

☆ Finally, see a beautiful butterfly hovering over your head. Hold your neck and shoulders, your chest and finally your abdomen motionless as the butterfly lands on each of them in turn, relaxing each part as the butterfly flutters downwards and away.

The Chakras

Chakras are psychic energy centres based at the cardinal points of the body. Opening these through visualisation is an effective method of preparing for psychic work, and can also be used to close down psychic channels.

The concept of chakras comes from the Hindu and Buddhist yogic tradition, although it has become increasingly popular in the West. The system I use focuses on seven

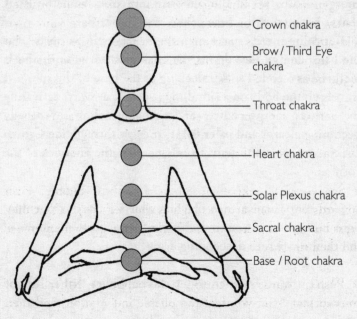

Crown chakra

Brow / Third Eye chakra

Throat chakra

Heart chakra

Solar Plexus chakra

Sacral chakra

Base / Root chakra

Your body and the chakras

chakras, but, according to the tradition followed, there are many variations in the number, sites and functions of chakras. The chakras, named after Sanskrit for wheel, are frequently pictured as whirling lotus petals of various colours. They are clear and turn harmoniously when mind, body and spirit are in tune.

You cannot see chakras physically, although Japanese experiments have found that the energy levels at the hypothesised locations of chakras of people who had worked in this field of spiritual development for years were measurably stronger than those of a control group.

The universal life force is said to enter through the Crown chakra at the top of the head and is filtered down through the other chakras, each of which transforms the energy into the appropriate form for the function it governs. Kundalini energy also passes in the opposite direction from the Root chakra situated at the base of the spine upwards.

Kundalini means snake or serpent power in Sanskrit. It is the basic energy that drives the chakras from within, and is pictured as a coiled snake sleeping at the base of the spine. It travels up the body on a spiralling psychic pathway, activating the various energy centres and changing colour, eventually becoming clearer and paler till it emerges through the Crown chakra as pure white light to mingle with the energies of the cosmos.

☆ You can visualise each of your whirling chakras opening, light rising within you and changing through the colours of the rainbow before descending again.

☆ There are no fixed energy paths or nadirs that hold true for everyone.

☆ You can also visualise the energies associated with the individual chakras as energising rays or coloured circles of light.

Chakra Colours

The Root Chakra, or Maladhara: The red chakra, the chakra of the Earth, is rooted at the base of the spine. It focuses on physical existence and survival. This is the chakra of courage and physical strength.

The Sacral Chakra, or Svadisthana: The orange chakra, the chakra of the Moon, is situated close to the genitals and reproductive system. It focuses on all aspects of physical satisfaction and is the home of the five senses. This is the chakra of all forms of fertility, needs and desires.

The Solar Plexus Chakra, or Manipura: The yellow chakra, the chakra of the Sun, is situated just above the navel around the solar plexus. It focuses on assimilating experiences. This is the chakra of power and determination or focused will.

The Heart Chakra, or Anahata: The green chakra, the chakra of the Four Winds, is situated centrally or slightly to the left of the chest, close to the heart. It focuses on emotions and sympathy. This is the chakra of love and relating to others.

The Throat Chakra, or Vishuddha: The blue chakra, the chakra of Time and Space, is situated close to the vocal chords in the centre of the neck. It focuses on ideas, ideals and clear communication. This is the chakra of truth and altruism.

The Third Eye/Brow Chakra, or Savikalpa Samadhi:
The purple chakra, the chakra of Freedom, is seated in the
centre of the brow, just above the eyes. It focuses on inspiration and psychic awareness. This is the chakra of connecting
with other dimensions.

The Crown Chakra, or Nirvakelpa Samadhi: The
white chakra, the chakra of Eternity, is situated at the centre
of the top of the head. It focuses on spiritual awareness and
unity with one's higher self. This is the chakra of wisdom and
understanding. It is a two-way chakra, since it receives light
from the cosmos.

Meditation and Psychic Awareness

Chakras are a very powerful way of reaching psychic levels of
functioning and awareness. Meditation is the process of
focusing on one thought, idea, image or even action while
excluding all other thoughts and actions. Everyone who has
fallen into a daydream or reverie – watching a bird, admiring
a flower, sitting by a fountain, or performing a rhythmic
action such as digging the garden, swaying to gentle music or
even vacuuming a patterned carpet – has experienced spontaneous meditation.

The prime effect of meditation is to create a heightened
state of awareness. Colours may seem brighter, the fragrance
of a flower quite overpowering and sounds not only heightened but transmuted, so that the distant roar of cars may
become a waterfall, a ringing telephone church bells.

Ideally you should meditate for 20 minutes or more a day.
But if you can only manage five or ten minutes a week before
physic work, it will still have the beneficial effect of stilling

tensions and switching your mind to the slower alpha rhythms that are the gateway to the unconscious. Alpha rhythms are an alternative state of consciousness in the brain entered during meditation, relaxation and spontaneously just as we are falling asleep or waking up. It is in this state that most creative spiritual work is done.

Using Mantras

A mantra is a phrase or a sound which is repeated rhythmically to help you enter and maintain a meditative state. The most basic and commonly used mantra or sound in meditative chanting is *Om* or *Aum*, said to be the sound of the universe, the sound that brought it into being. However you can use any rhythmic, resounding word as a focus.

Intone or think the mantra each time you breathe out.

Beginning Meditation

Sit or lie comfortably, as you did for relaxation. If you are using a focus, place the object so that you can see it without moving your neck or head. Experiment with positioning it at different heights and distances until you feel comfortable. A natural focus is best, such as a plant, a flower, or a small indoor water feature (you can easily make one with a deep container, a very small electric pump and some plants).

☆ See yourself surrounded by a circle of warm, protective light.

☆ Let this circle expand and contract until you are bathed in it but can see quite clearly through it to your focus.

☆ If you have no external focus, close your eyes and focus on the circle of light within.

☆ Alternatively, direct your gaze to a spot on the wall, perhaps a silver or gold circle you have hung on a cord or painted there.

☆ Concentrate on your breathing, taking a slow deep breath through your nose and slowly exhaling through your mouth.

☆ Let the focus, whether an external object or a single word, phrase or thought, expand and fill your mind, so that all other sights, sounds and sensations recede.

☆ If you have a meditation mantra, repeat the word slowly in your mind each time you exhale and let the sound echo as you inhale successive breaths.

☆ Hold the thought, word or image for about five minutes, repeating the word or letting the colour and form of the object flow through you so that you become the flower or the colour.

☆ After a while you will find yourself gradually moving away from the focus, letting the image or thought fade.

☆ As you do this, external sounds will return and your normal range of vision expand.

Focused Action

Spontaneous meditative states come while carrying out a repetitive physical action. In times gone by women at the wash tub would often see prophetic images in the suds. Sages would manipulate yarrow stalks from one hand to the other, while allowing their minds to slow down and open psychically to receive the wisdom of the I Ching. Repetitive action – even hard labour – can have a soothing effect. Our ancestors, who spent a great deal of time on routine repetitive tasks, had far harder lives but surely did not suffer the angst or stress-related disorders of modern life.

Meditation through routine actions should be induced deliberately only where there is no machinery or danger. For example, digging a small patch of earth with a trowel while sitting on grass is an appropriate time to meditate, but trying this while driving a powered lawnmower could be dangerous. Other good examples include rubbing together fat and flour for pastry in a large bowl, winding a ball of wool (another folk ritual used in traditional love spells), scattering grass seeds or shelling peas. The more useful the action, the more likely the psyche is to be lulled into a light trance, safe in the knowledge that you cannot be accused of time-wasting and daydreaming.

☆ Let your mind go blank and concentrate on the action so that you become part of it.

☆ The physical rhythm will carry your mind to a deeper level of awareness. On stopping, you may find that an image, word or phrase comes unbidden into your mind. This will answer a question you had only half-formulated, but which is central to your current well-being.

Creative Visualisation

Visualisation differs from meditation because it uses an image or focus for a pre-determined purpose. It harnesses the little used but valuable imaging processes that underpin all forms of divination and psychic work generally. This is the power that transforms an ink blot floating on water or a tea leaf in a cup into a meaningful image from our deep unconscious that may hold the key to a dilemma.

Visualisation comes naturally to children and for people in those few remaining societies which have not been invaded by technology. As adults we no longer so readily think in pictures; we have become accustomed to verbalising and in a sense restricting our creativity to what can be explained, rather than felt instinctively or seen clairvoyantly.

If you can develop these natural innate imaging powers, clairvoyant abilities and predictive abilities develop almost as a by-product. You can also harness these image-making abilities for other forms of divination such as using Tarot cards or runes. At these times, you will see not only images related to the symbols emerging in the individual cards or runes, but associated visions that link them to the present or future of the person for whom you are reading.

Visualisation also expands the bounds of possibility to encompass all the senses. If you can visualise a need, you can use this power to make dreams into reality and transform thoughts into action.

☆ Begin by picturing something you need. Like all psychic senses, visualisation operates most powerfully in the sphere of human emotions and real wants.

☆ Focus on this need. Some people use a tangible focus: a postcard of a resort or country you wish to visit, a photo of someone you love from whom you are estranged, a brochure of a car or house you want. Be as specific as possible – colour and make of car, type of dwelling and location.

☆ Whether you use an external focus or rely solely on your

internal imagery, picture the desired state or possession in your mind's eye, calling on all your senses, to make the image three-dimensional.

☆ Concentrate on details. When you are ready, create in your mind's vision the symbol of whatever it is you want.

☆ Go through every step, savouring the emotions at every stage from initial anxiety to the pleasure of bringing the scheme to fruition.

☆ If a need is complex you may need to repeat the visualisation several times, embellishing the details, so that each time it becomes closer to the projected reality.

☆ You may find that during your visualisation a deeper level takes over and that you see your new house or lover in an unexpected location. You may see clues that will be of help in the outside world.

☆ You can build into any visualisation a short-cut back to these feelings of happiness or assurance of success to be used in the future by saying a phrase such as: 'When I touch my hair or squeeze my arm gently, I will recall the joy, calm or assurance of success I am feeling now.'

☆ When you have finished your visualisation, begin to turn your dreams into reality by taking the first steps towards your goal. Psychic powers can offer a tremendous impetus to success or happiness, but we cannot rely on them alone. Dreams need to be brought into the outer world if your psychic awareness is to make your life happier or richer in every way.

EXERCISE: COPING WITH UNPLEASANT SITUATIONS

Learning to relax in the peace and quiet of your home is just one step on the road you have begun to travel. Your meditation and relaxation techniques can be effective when dealing with someone who is being difficult, perhaps a colleague, a truculent relation, a nosy neighbour or petty official. Before replying to them with a burst of anger – which is as dangerous to you as it is to them, because it raises your stress levels – begin breathing for a minute. This will allow you to keep control of your emotions if he or she is in mid-tirade or you anticipate a barbed criticism or piece of malice. As you exhale, visualise this aggressive or obstructive figure swaddled in a pink cotton wool blanket and silently and gently recite as your mantra, 'Go in peace.' Your silence and calm will be very disarming. The assailant may be distracted by it, stop in mid-flow and turn away.

Try creating visualisations in advance for different stressful situations, making mantras for meditations, depending on the circumstances.

2

Psychic Protection

Psychic protection is a process that over time becomes as automatic as switching off the lights or checking that the car is locked. It is needed primarily not to avoid picking up unpleasant entities or dark energies in your psychic work, but to prevent your own psyche from being overwhelmed by the vast number of impressions you will receive from other people and the natural world.

Healers and those who do psychic work are highly receptive and frequently deal with the problems and fears of others. Because of this, they often absorb negative feelings that can, if unchecked, spill over into their own lives. Moreover, some people, without intending, can be emotional and psychic vampires, draining energies from others. We all have a colleague or friend who comes to visit, invariably full of woes, resentments and negativity; when he or she leaves, they feel refreshed having poured out their troubles, but we are left drained and depressed on their behalf. Even without such people, the most positive psychic work can leave our senses buzzing all night.

Some people insist that following elaborate pre-ordained

rituals, usually taken wholesale from a book or teacher, will automatically confer total immunity from all harm. My own experience and extensive research has shown that personally developed methods, rather than those of other people, are most helpful in drawing boundaries around your psychic work and symbolically excluding any negativity, whether emanating from yourself or others. For this reason the following suggestions for psychic protection should be regarded only as ideas and basic formats. You can adapt these to your own needs and feelings so that they become endowed with your own unique protective and healing powers and those of your higher self or guardian spirits.

No protection, however powerful, can be effective if people dabble with black magic or try to summon up unearthly entities. Whether the demons that can be unleashed are psychic or psychological, they are uncontrollable and fatal.

Psychic protection is two-fold: firstly, it offers peace of mind for explorations into our own deeper awareness; secondly, it protects us not from demons but those living people who feel malevolent towards us and who consciously or unconsciously send negative thoughts our way.

The golden rules are:

☆ Do not try to harness powers other than those of the natural world and your own inner energies.

☆ Do not use a ouija board.

☆ Do not call down spirits into the candle flame or hold seances in which you summon the dead. Talking to a beloved mother or grandfather who has departed in a positive, gentle way or tuning into the energies of the past in an old building is very different from trying to invoke ghosts or spirits as a way of demonstrating psychic power or seeking to obtain information for self-interest.

☆ Mediumship involving contacting the deceased on behalf of others should be attempted only in a controlled situation with the help of a trained medium (addresses for initial contacts of training circles are given at page 144). I have encountered very gifted psychics who were almost driven insane by thinking that they could control spirits, send demons against enemies or manipulate magical powers.

☆ If you ever feel that you are becoming obsessed to the exclusion of the everyday world, that your mind is being controlled by outside forces, earthly or otherwise, or that you cannot close down your psychic energies, that is the time to stop and concentrate on practical, earthly activities such as gardening, decorating or doing your household accounts.

☆ If you still feel overwhelmed, seek advice from an experienced healer and medium.

☆ Like all gifts, psychic powers are not intrinsically good or evil but can be used for either positive or negative intents. You may instantly sense a psychic group or individual who has darkness all around them. Avoid them and contact one of the reputable organisations, either Christian or pagan, for reliable and benign contacts. (Pagan is from the Latin *paganus* which simply means 'country dweller'. Paganism is an umbrella term for all people who celebrate the natural world.)

☆ The greatest protection is to work only with positive intent and never when you are angry, exhausted or anxious.

Exercise, thump a pillow or watch a funny film until you are restored, as bad feelings will naturally tinge what you are doing. Many so-called poltergeist intrusions are reflections of our own unresolved resentments fuelled by our innate psychic powers.

Guardian Angels, Archangels and Protective Guides

These benevolent spirits offer the most traditional form of psychic protection and, for some people, provide a specific focus for benign forces of light and love. Some people invoke angels to stand in each corner of the room; others a single guardian. These can be traditional angels with golden wings or personal guides you may have encountered in dreams and past-life work – a sage, a nun, an Ancient Egyptian priest, a priestess from Atlantis or a kindly deceased grandmother who, you sense, watches over you.

We all conceptualise or experience protection in our own way and your own guardian, however homely, is more effective than a formal evocation of an archangel to whom you may not directly relate.

When you have finished your psychic work, silently thank your protector(s) and, because you have taken protection from the cosmos, restore the balance with a small positive act towards someone in need of care – feed wild birds, scatter a few seeds in an unloved area of land, make a friendly phone call or write an encouraging letter to someone who is lonely or who has been unpleasant to you through personal unhappiness.

Visualisation of Light

If you find that the concept of a personified guardian does not suit you, try envisaging cosmic protection as pure white or golden light.

☆ Picture pure white, golden or yellow light encircling you.

☆ An egg or spherical shape enclosing the entire body is best, drawn in your mind's eye clockwise from above the head in an unbroken circle.

☆ If you are working with someone else, create a separate force field of light round them so that you do not absorb any of the doubts or sorrows they may generate during psychic work.

☆ Draw another clockwise circle of light around any divinatory devices you are using.

☆ Let the shell of the protective sphere harden into an iridescent mother-of-pearl shield so that only loving thoughts may enter. Any negative feelings from whatever source will be sent back to the originator.

☆ You can place a protective shell of light around those you love at any time they seem vulnerable. Use a soft pink light for children and animals and a purple one for older people.

☆ You can also enclose your house or car if you need to leave it unattended for a while.

☆ Use a soft grey shell if you are travelling alone late at night or in an unfamiliar place to give you added protection beyond the physical precautions you take.

Instant Protection

Once it has been initially created, the psychic shell of light is always there at a distance. When not in use, it merely fades into the background. If you feel you need instant protection, you can create a short cut to summon up this shell immediately by associating it with a symbol (see Chapter 1 for more information on meditation and visualisation). This can be used against general negativity and also if you are handling any objects in psychometry that give off negative vibes or if you visit a place for clairsentience or clairvoyance that feels unfriendly.

☆ Create or use any symbolic action or tangible focus that works for you. For example, you could trace a clockwise sphere on your left hand or in the air around an amulet that might be a lucky charm, a St Christopher medallion, a silver locket or crystal worn around your neck or on your wrist. These symbols work best if they are associated with positive memories or feelings such as happiness and love.

☆ You may find it useful to affirm either silently or out loud the first few times you are setting up the link between the psychic shield and the symbol, with words such as: 'When I draw this sphere, my shell of light will protect me.'

☆ You can repeat this affirmation each night before you go to sleep so that you are safe from negative thoughts while you are sleeping.

A *Psychic Force Field*

Should you sense particularly strong hostility from someone you meet, or feel a particular person at home or work is chipping at your self-confidence, you can make the edge of your shell or shield stronger by activating your natural force field, also known as your psychic electric fence.

This force is part of the auric field, the psychic energy that is believed to emanate a few inches around people, animals and even plants. With practice, this aura can be seen as a spectrum of rainbow colours, according to our health and well-being.

Even without a study of auras you can use this natural defence mechanism to keep out intrusions of all kinds. Pictures of saints have sparks emanating from their haloes. These represent the energy fields that we all possess and that we can use to mark our personal limits.

☆ Shake your fingertips until you can feel the energy flowing.

☆ Hold your hands about 15cm apart, fingers spread wide open, palms facing each other.

☆ Slowly bring your hands together until they touch.

☆ Repeat the exercise two or three times.

☆ You may feel a warmth or heaviness around your hands as you bring them closer together.

☆ When you are aware of this sensation, hold your hands in the same position, again about 15cm apart.

☆ Bring your hands together so that they nearly touch, move them apart, then move them back together. Continue this for five or six cycles.

☆ As well as intensifying the energy, you may perceive greyish bands of light around your fingers and between your hands.

☆ As you move your hands, see the light becoming brighter and clearer and creating sparks or rays.

☆ Extend these sparks from your left hand so that they move clockwise upwards in the shape of the golden sphere around your body until they join with your right hand.

☆ The sparks from your right hand will travel clockwise downwards around your body, tracing the edge of the sphere, and join with those rising from your left hand.

☆ Picture the sparks as a golden zig-zag in yellows and orange, not in any way harmful, but gently repelling any negativity.

☆ You can also trace this force field around your body with a clear crystal quartz glinting in the sunlight if you are alone.

☆ If you are in company or at work and see the office gossip or a critical boss coming your way, draw a doodle on paper of the ellipse with a figure inside, surrounded by sparks. You will discover they veer away or are less strident than usual. They may stop, looking puzzled before withdrawing rapidly.

Protective Crystals

Certain crystals have natural protective powers. Choose one or two from the suggestions below and position them either in the corners of the room or the four corners of the table where you are working.

☆ A clear quartz or amethyst pyramid placed in front of you during psychic work or on an office desk will absorb any approaching negativity.

☆ Use a protective crystal on a chain or cord around your neck, in a ring or on a bracelet to act as a shield from any harm. The circular shape of these settings offers additional security.

☆ Alternatively carry a defensive crystal in your bag or pocket.

☆ Protective crystals traditionally include: black agate, amethyst, bloodstone, carnelian, garnet, black and red jasper, jet, lapis lazuli, obsidian, rose quartz, smoky quartz, sodalite, tiger's eye, topaz and turquoise.

If you have a personal crystal that has become endowed with positive healing energies, this will be equally effective as your personal guardian.

Preparing and Cleansing Your Protective Crystals

One of the simplest but most effective methods of purification is to invoke the symbolism of the ancient elements of Earth, Air, Fire and Water that the ancient Greeks once believed to be the building blocks of the universe. These elements are still regarded as focuses for the energies of the natural world and, according to the psychologist Carl Gustav Jung, represent aspects of our psyche: Earth represents sensation, Air thought, Fire intuition and Water feeling.

☆ Before use, sprinkle your protective crystals with sea salt for the security and grounding of Earth.

☆ Next pass your crystals through the smoke of – or waft over them – an incense stick or oil burner with a cleansing fragrance such as juniper or pine for the logic and courage of Air.

☆ Pass the crystals through or over a candle flame of gold or yellow for the clear vision and inspiration of Fire.

☆ Finally sprinkle over the crystals rose water for love or pure spring water for the innate sensitivity and adaptability of Water.

☆ After use, wash your protective crystals in running water. If you have been in contact with a particularly negative person, leave the crystals for a few days with a large piece of amethyst or rose quartz, either in water or wrapped in a dark cloth.

☆ Alternatively, pass a clear crystal pendulum anti-clock-wise over the crystals slowly nine times, seeing dark, misty negative powers rising upwards and being absorbed by the pendulum. Cleanse your pendulum under running water.

Protective Herbs, Oils and Incense

Essential Oils

You can burn a protective oil before or after psychic work or if you have a visitor who drains your energies. Powerful protective burning oils include: cedarwood, cypress, peppermint, pine, rosemary, sage or thyme.

If possible, relax yourself before psychic exploration by having a bath in a gently protective oil – no more than ten drops in all. This can be especially healing if you have gathered any tensions earlier in the day. Protective bath oils include: rose, geranium, lavender or sandalwood.

Herbal Protection

Bay, basil, lavender, parsley or rose are considered particularly effective for protection. Make an infusion of one of them by adding two or three teaspoons of crushed fresh or dried leaves or flowers to a cup of boiling water for ten minutes before straining.

☆ Sprinkle a few drops of the cooled mixture in the corners of a room where you will be carrying out spiritual work.

☆ Do the same in a bedroom for quiet sleep after psychic work or a stressful day.

☆ Sprinkle a few drops across the threshold of a room to prevent hostility entering.

You can also use the infusion to cleanse every room, beginning at the front door and then working from the top of the house down if there have been any domestic upheavals that have left bad feelings or unresolved conflict.

Tip any remaining infusion out of the back door, or a back window if you live in an apartment.

Incense

Burning incense is a natural prelude to psychic work. The incenses that seem to induce psychic awareness carry with them natural in-built protection. Use either cones, sticks or a small incense charcoal burner. You can also burn protective incenses after psychic work or to remove any lingering emotions, especially negative ones.

They are also a good way of cleansing a home of bad temper or unfair criticism that has engendered resentment and hurt. My favourite defensive incenses are: cedar, dragon's blood, frankincense, gum arabic, juniper, myrrh and sandalwood.

Closing Down Your Energies

One of the most effective ways of marking the end of a concentrated period of psychic exploration is to have a transition period in which you tidy and put away equipment, wash out bowls you may have used for scrying (see page 67), sweep up any ash or herbs you have scattered and cleanse crystals under water. You are not shedding your psychic awareness, merely marking the passage to another stage in the day where different energies will come to the fore or you will rest.

☆ Putting everything away in your treasure box and closing the lid is a physical signal that you are moving this aspect of your world to one side for a while.

☆ Having a simple meal or drink with friends who have shared psychic work allows you gradually to revert your energies back to the everyday sphere. For this reason food and drink were always a part of the traditional seasonal agricultural festivals and still have a place in more formal religion, for example the Harvest Supper.

☆ The simplest method involves washing your hands and splashing your face with pure spring water from a glass container in which a clear crystal quartz has been kept. The glass container should have been left standing for a full 24-hour period, preferably in sun and waxing or full moonlight, although the waning moon is potent for banishing energies.

☆ Before washing, some people make the sign of the cross in the water, either the Christian cross or the diagonally armed astrological sign for the Earth that is still seen on hot cross buns, as an additional protective measure.

☆ Do not dry your hands and face, but shake the water off your hands and let them dry naturally.

☆ Empty the remaining water into the earth, either the garden or a flowerpot or window box.

☆ Refill the bowl with pure spring water.

☆ Finally circle a clear quartz crystal pendulum nine times above your head anti-clockwise to remove any lingering negativity or free-floating psychic energies.

☆ See your protective shell of light fade gently, but be aware it is always there if you need it, as are your intuitive powers.

Closing the Chakras

If you find the concept of chakras described in Chapter 1 helpful, you can end a period of psychic work by closing down the energy centres that you have opened for the free flow of spiritual power and inspiration and the interchange of energies with earth and sky.

☆ Visualise the whirling chakra petals becoming much slower, so that they are turning gently and in harmony, as the pure cosmic spiritual energy flows down the body and the colours merge naturally into each other.

☆ Begin with the Crown chakra at the top of your head and quieten the whirling petals, so that the pure white light becomes mistier and eventually moves downwards to join the purple energy at the Third Eye chakra, situated in the middle of your brow. Your thoughts are stilled.

☆ Let the Third Eye or Brow chakra also become lulled and the rich purple merge into first a deep and then a paler blue as the light moves downwards to your Throat chakra.

☆ The Throat chakra too becomes tranquil as blue transforms into turquoise and eventually green as it reaches the Heart chakra, in the centre of the chest. You can feel your heart rate slowing to a gentle regular beat.

☆ The green moves downwards to merge with the yellow of the Solar Plexus chakra just above the navel, which also becomes quieter as the digestive system rests.

☆ The light will become orange as it moves still lower to the

Sacral chakra, situated centrally below the navel, close to your reproductive system. Desires and hungers fade and the power descends until you have a slightly warm heaviness at the base of your spine.

☆ Here the energy is deep red and this Kundalini or Root chakra energy coils, sleeping but always alert, like a battery recharging or a generator without calls on its stored power.

☆ If you are going to bed, now your system is quiet, draw over yourself in your mind's eye a pink fluffy cotton wool cloud, like a sleeping bag zipped over your head so you are quite safe as you rest or sleep.

☆ If this is difficult, hold as a focus between your hands a chunk of uncut and unpolished rose quartz and enter into its cloudy, calm depths.

EXERCISE: CREATING A PROTECTIVE BOTTLE

One of the oldest domestic protective rituals, practised especially among older folk on both sides of the Atlantic, involves a small dark glass bottle and a mass of threads, wool and embroidery silks. Children love this activity.

☆ Fill a raffia basket with different coloured wools, silks, threads, even pieces of string. Place it beside the bottle or jar, which should contain a pinch of salt for healing.

☆ If there are small children you may wish to precut the threads into lengths of 8–9cm, but otherwise leave scissors next to the basket.

☆ When a person returns home worried, angry or resentful, get him or her to cut a short length of thread to represent a bad feeling then place it in the bottle.

☆ If a knot is tied in the thread the energy is bound and can be transformed into positive protective power.

☆ Use separate threads for individual problems or frustration – five minutes spent filling the jar works wonders for stress levels.

☆ As each piece is added to the bottle or jar, the person should say:

Tangle the wool,
Heal the anger,
Keep me safe,
From every danger.

☆ This is only one version of a ritual whose variations formed part of the traditions of family life that died out with increasing urbanisation and the decline of the extended family. These old rhymes and rituals encouraged spontaneous psychic powers.

☆ When the bottle is full, add a sprig of fresh or a pinch of dried rosemary for transforming negativity into healing power, seal the bottle and keep it in a high place.

☆ Begin a new bottle and when that is completed, throw the old one away. That way you keep your home positive and the protective energies renewed.

3

Psychometry

'Many of us have keepsakes, things of no monetary value, but sentimental and nostalgic mementoes which stimulate our memories and are reminders of sequences of events within our own lives. Old photographs, letters, coins, buttons, tickets, programmes, certificates or holiday souvenirs. Individually they may seem small and insignificant but put them together in an imaginative way and we have a way of communicating that "I was here. I did this. I learned that. I did and do exist."' – Yvonne Malik, who creates memory boxes of personal memorabilia for bereaved people to commemorate the lives of deceased family members.

If you have ever entered a house and decided immediately that it 'felt right', or chosen a piece of jewellery or a car for the same reason and been well pleased with your purchase, then you have already used psychometry, the art of picking up impressions from inanimate objects. As it is a natural talent, it is a good entry point into psychic development.

In some people, this ability is developed to a startling extent. An expert psychometrist can, for example, pick up a brooch and relate facts about the present and previous owners. A good palmist constantly touches the palm of a client and frequently gains more information from the energies he or she feels pulsating in the hand than by adhering to the conventional meaning of the lines.

Using an Object to Pick Up Psychic Impressions

Psychometric work does not demand that we use a valuable work of art or a Roman coin. The best psychometry involves touching objects to which great sentimental value is attached, for example a family ring or necklace, an old photograph or ornament that has passed through different generations of the same family. A teapot around which family and friends have gathered in joy and sorrow over decades can hold a whole treasure house of psychic impressions. Psychic abilities operate best through the channel of human emotions.

Many experiences occur quite spontaneously. Sue from Pennsylvania found her grandmother's jewellery was still watched over by the old lady ten years after her death:

> My grandmother died, but only after ten years were the contents of her home sorted out. My mother collected several small pieces of jewellery, nothing of more than sentimental value. Her intention was to give each of us a piece of jewellery.
>
> Some time later when I went home for a visit, I asked my sister whether she would rather have the bracelet or the earrings. She said, 'Take both, I don't want either'. I was shocked and confused. She told me that during the summer, as she was working in the kitchen, she would see a shadow out of the corner of her eye. Her first

impression was that it was the cat jumping up on the counter (something the cat did not ordinarily do). When my sister turned to chase it, the cat would not be there. At night she began to hear what she called deliberate knocks and thumps in the house. We had both grown up in this house and were familiar with all the normal noises that it made.

One day my mother told my sister, 'You are going to think I'm crazy, but I've been seeing shadows all around the house. When I turn to face them, nothing is there!' It appeared they were experiencing exactly the same thing.

Since these things started to happen after my mother took the jewellery, we all felt that it was definitely connected. Even though my sister was uncomfortable keeping any of it, I took the bracelet and left the earrings. Once we each had something the disturbances stopped. We can only surmise that my grandmother wanted to make certain that she approved of the way her jewellery was divided and wanted me to have the bracelet.

Few people will detect the presence of a previous owner of jewellery as vividly as Sue and her family. However, most people instinctively sense impressions from the past or strong emotions that are not connected with their own immediate feelings if they handle either a family treasure or touch the stone walls at a ruined castle or ancient monument.

How Psychometry Works

Two theories explain psychometry, neither of which excludes the other. The most powerful and accurate psychometric impressions may occur when both channels are open.

Psychometry of the Place

The history of the object itself or its place of origin may be the focus. If an article has remained in the same family for generations, it can retain a whole family history, just as a gramophone record holds music or words within its grooves. Objects from sites of antiquity seem to absorb physical and emotional imprints from those who have lived in the place, trodden its paths or halls and visited over the years. The strongest impressions from place psychometry result from dramatic or violent events – such as murders or battles – or the experience of long periods of unbroken tranquillity, such as the case of an abbey where monks may have lived over a period of hundreds of years in the same pattern so that their individual lifespans run into one.

Clairsentience, sensing an atmosphere, is closely akin to psychometry, as is clairaudience, hearing voices from the past. These are frequently part of a psychometric experience, triggered by touch. Clairvoyance, seeing figures or scenes from the past, can also be stimulated by a psychometric experience. For many people it is through psychometry that these related psychic abilities first emerge.

Psychometry of Current Experience and Concerns

An article can also be used to transmit information not about its own history but about the past, present and future of the person who currently owns the object. In this second kind of psychometry, the artefact is acting as a transmitter of psychic information in the same way as a crystal ball or Tarot cards channel the intuitive impressions conveyed from subject to seer.

Both forms of psychometry can occur simultaneously, but usually one predominates according to the nature of the item and the purpose of the reading. If you visit an old site and touch the stones you will probably learn more about the place than about your present dilemmas or those of anyone else present. However, if you are holding a friend's grand-mother's ring, you may sense not only the story of the ring but unvoiced concerns from your friend about her own life, transmitted from her psyche to yours via the ring. Frequently these dilemmas echo events in the life of a previous owner.

The newer or less personal the object, the more you will pick up about the enquirer rather than the artefact.

Beginning Psychometry

The greatest problem when beginning psychometry is to learn to trust your instincts. Initially if you identify objects by feel and not visually, you can shut out the temptation to rely on logical processes that will automatically start to make deductions about the age and likely ownership of the artefact.

☆ Ask a friend to bring you an item that is at least 20 years old – preferably much older – that is of sentimental value to their family.

☆ Place it in a covered box so that you cannot see it.

☆ Do not ask the other person to hold the object. Initially you are concentrating on the history of the item.

☆ Ask your friend to leave you alone while you experiment so that you do not feel pressurised to succeed at this early stage (this can lead to guessing).

☆ With your eyes closed, put your hands in the box and hold the article between cupped hands without trying to identify it too precisely.

☆ Move your palms and your fingertips gently over the surface, probing any indentations, still with your eyes closed.

☆ Do not force impressions. Let colours, sounds, even scenes emerge over a period of minutes.

☆ You may feel yourself moving inside the object so that it encloses you, much as a crystal-ball reader projects his- or herself within the glass sphere.

☆ The object will gradually feel warmer. This is a common feature of psychometry and shows that you are making contact at a significant level.

☆ If you sense nothing, keep fingering the object, seeing it in your mind's eye in a setting, which may not be one that you might expect. If you have recognised the object previously you may have unconsciously put it into an expected context.

During an early attempt at psychometry, Pauline, one of my pupils, kept seeing what felt like a tiny porcelain figure surrounded by crowds of people crammed into a cold metal container splashed by the sea. She discovered that it was a figure of a Dresden shepherdess which had belonged to a soldier involved in the D-Day landings. He had carried it throughout the war as a talisman. The container had been a landing craft and the soldier's granddaughter also used the tiny figurine as her lucky charm – and was engaged to be married to a sailor.

☆ Gradually move back from the object to view in your

imagination a table on which the object was standing at its most significant time. Note the room and any people in the room.

☆ You may chose to follow one of the people, noting clothes, furnishings and words.

☆ The imagination is the doorway to the psyche, so do not worry that you are making up facts.

☆ When you are receiving no new impressions, open your eyes.

☆ Ask your friend what he or she knows of the history. If the information you have received does not seem to tally, it does not mean you have failed.

Further enquiries may reveal that the pictures relate to another person who owned the artefact; questions to older family friends can often provide answers or clues, and you will be surprised at your own accuracy in this initial foray. Articles can pass through many hands in even a comparatively short number of years, so you may never be able to prove your theory. But in the elusive field of the psychic, demands for hard proof can sometimes overlook the magical insights into a past era.

Developing Object Psychometry

The basic technique for all object psychometry is described above. Once you start to read for friends and acquaintances, you will find it more natural to look at the item that you are holding.

☆ As you do so, describe out loud your impressions, however unlikely, without trying to rationalise them.

☆ Keep talking rather than pausing to ask if the information is correct. This can interrupt the flow and destroy confidence if the other person hesitates or questions your feelings.

☆ Recording the sessions means that you can discuss the details afterwards and have a record to check against family archives or with older relations.

☆ While you are concentrating on perfecting object psychometry do not ask the person to hold the object, as this may introduce personal information about their current lives and dilemmas. Eventually you will happily run the two kinds of psychometry – objects and owners – in tandem.

Psychometry of the Place

Begin at a place of recognised antiquity, an old stone circle, a burial mound or a ruined castle where you can pick up stones or old pottery and hold them. Many industrial museums have reconstructed buildings in which you can sit and touch furniture, pots or disused machinery. If a site has been stripped back to its bones, psychometry may be easier than in an elaborately furnished stately home with artefacts from many different places that have not shared the life of the house. Sometimes a very detailed reconstruction of a period that centres on the lives of the noble and famous can blur the richer vein that may be composed of the lives of ordinary people who worked as servants over centuries.

☆ If the house or castle is furnished, try to use any furniture that has been in the house for centuries.

☆ Do not research the history, but let your impressions form as you touch the walls or an object that attracts you.

☆ Throughout the experience, maintain tactile contact with the artefact or building.

☆ A particular era may predominate in the images you see or sounds you hear in your mind's ear. Later research may show that this is usually a time when dramatic events occurred on the site.

☆ If possible, visit early in the day or the hour before closing, so that you can be undisturbed and perhaps sit in an alcove or on a seat, touching an original piece of panelling or an arrow slit in the outer wall.

☆ Run your hands over and around it. Note the texture on a conscious level – rough, smooth, cold, hard, and then feel the object getting warmer.

☆ Look now inside the stone or object, using your mind's eye. You may wish to close your eyes.

☆ Accept the first image or sound that comes. Let images flow, however disjointed, until the jigsaw falls into place.

☆ As you continue to make physical contact, let your inner vision move beyond the artefact, as in your earlier experiments, and allow the owner to appear before you either in words or as a sudden image, either externally or in your inner psyche.

☆ You may be surprised by the person or people you see. Sometimes someone along the road of history became attached to a place or object and made a strong imprint that will over-ride the original owner or inhabitants. Henry VIII, for example, because of the strength of his personality, is a frequent visitor to many stately homes in the south of England.

☆ Afterwards look round the immediate area to discover clues to locations you saw psychometrically. Study carefully any portraits and read not only the guidebook about the property, but visit a museum of local history where you may find legends, old maps and even lists of servants.

Often a chat to the curator and a very detailed history of the building can explain a sudden despair or fear experienced when you touched objects in a certain room, as there may have been a murder or a siege. Many curators will not be surprised at your questions and usually have tales of their own of strange happenings that have occurred on the spot you identified. You may even uncover a priest hole or secret doorway by touching a panel and experiencing sudden urgency and the need to hide (see also Chapter 4 on clairsentience).

Personal Psychometry

This forms a potent alternative to more conventional divinatory methods such as Tarot or runes. It offers, especially where issues are complex, insight into the links between past events and future action in the life of an individual.

☆ Hold a personal object such as a ring, watch, necklace or a key ring belonging to someone with whom you are at ease. The item need not be particularly old, but if it has sentimental value this will increase the emotional energy that enhances psychic transmission.

☆ With all forms of personal psychometry, you will usually progress from the past through the present and future concerns of a person.

☆ Childhood scenes are most common, perhaps because at that time the psychic world is at its strongest, and so they are the most easily retrievable through psychometry (and other psychic work).

☆ Ask the person for whom you are reading to hold their possession for a few moments while they concentrate on any questions or dilemmas that are causing concern.

☆ Hold the article between you so that the joint psychic vibes from you and the other person mingle within the artefact.

☆ Finally touch the object yourself with your eyes closed, if that makes psychic focusing easier.

☆ Run your fingertips and your palms over the surface for a few minutes.

☆ As you become more practised you will be able to distinguish whether a picture relates to the distant or more recent past.

☆ Reading the future is the most important aspect of any

personal psychic reading, as it is usually concerns about the future that have prompted the enquirer to seek a reading. What you are seeing are potential paths. The key to becoming a good reader is to present these possibilities as positive options so that the enquirer feels totally in control of his or her destiny and confident about that future, however many obstacles lie in the way.

A SAMPLE PSYCHOMETRIC READING

Julie was in her early twenties and had just graduated from college. She planned to spend a year working in a bar in Spain, improving her Spanish and having a good time before starting a career in accountancy. However, her parents insisted that she should establish herself in her profession, save for a house and settle down rather than dropping out after her years of education.

Julie gave Lin, an experienced psychometrist, a fan that had belonged to her great-grandmother, who came to England from Spain at the turn of the century to marry Julie's great-grandfather, a sailor from the industrial North. She had never returned to Spain and there were no relatives with whom the family kept in contact. Lin knew none of this, only that the fan had been in the family for many years.

Lin held the fan and saw a vivid dark green tree, full of oranges, brown goats and a bare-footed dark-skinned teenager running laughing after the goats which had escaped into a potato field. Then the goats were on the shore and a boatload of sailors rowed on to the beach. The girl was seized, bound and gagged, bundled into the boat, and returned to a huge wooden ship driven by steam, where she was locked in a dark, dirty hold. Lin heard screams of terror as the girl was attacked again and again and at last cast ashore at Liverpool docks. Then there was nothing but darkness, hands pulling her upwards. The darkness cleared to be replaced by impressions of a wedding to a much older man.

The subsequent greyness was broken only by the vivid colour of the fan and a girl, now prematurely a woman and mother, dancing the flamencos she had loved as a young girl when no one was around. Then the dance was stilled.

Lin had uncovered a family secret, one Julie's family were unwilling to discuss but which she confirmed from parish records of the marriage of her Spanish great-grandmother and a man 35 years older, an undertaker by trade. What was vital for Julie was the certainty that now she should seek her happiness in the land of her great-grandmother and perhaps learn the old songs and dances.

Julie did visit Spain and understood her underlying heritage. She returned many times in later years drawn to what was a natural and important part of herself.

EXERCISE: PSYCHOMETRY WITH COMPARATIVE STRANGERS

Once you have used informal psychometry with friends you will find that other people for readings. Carry out as many as possible, recording your results in your psychic journal. Before long you will find that impressions come much faster and with great accuracy, even when you are not trying.

Then you can move on to colleagues and comparative strangers. You will need to be very subtle, but opportunities naturally arise when you can admire a book, hold a bunch of keys casually as you talk or run your fingers gently along a fine piece of antique furniture. You may pick up impressions of the history of the artefact or about the owner.

Gradually insert your psychic information into the conversation, making enquiries about the origins of an article or holiday plans or family background, to confirm your intuitive insights.

If someone seems troubled, psychometry can help you to ask the right questions and offer relevant advice.

4

Clairsentience

Clairsentience can be defined as the psychic ability, akin to intuition, that relies on the sixth sense to gain impressions of places and people not available to the conscious mind. The most common example is an ability to sense a strange atmosphere on entering a house. This ability requires no physical contact with artefacts, as does psychometry, but may reveal itself as a general uneasiness, the prickling of hairs on the back of a neck or a distinct feeling of coldness. Clairsentience can then trigger clairvoyant or clairaudient experiences. Some people see former inhabitants either in the mind's eye or externally. Some people use clairsentience and follow it with psychometry to draw upon all the psychic senses.

The majority of clairsentient experiences are positive. Houses can retain happy atmospheres of former inhabitants, living as well as dead. Some exude a constant sense of peace. After a family member has died, relatives may sense the calm, loving presence of the deceased person around the former home immediately after the funeral, on anniversaries or at times of sadness. By far the majority of family ghosts are experienced in this way, rather than seen or heard.

Such experiences are usually spontaneous, but it is quite possible to tune into places and into the essence of people we have loved who have died by visiting places where we shared happy memories with them. Ann, who is a book editor, described her clairsentient experiences to me after working on a manuscript I had sent her about ghosts:

My partner and I had been house-hunting for some months when we found and fell in love with a 16th-century cottage in the tiny Kentish village where I spent much of my childhood. It was a pretty cottage and from the moment we walked in, we knew we must have it. We moved in and set about making it cosy. We decided to revamp the bathroom as it was shabby and always felt cold, and we replaced the sitting-room floor, running the central heating pipes beneath it to draw attention to the lovely old beams.

Just before Christmas, I kept mislaying things at the very moment I needed them, finding them some time later just where they were originally meant to be. Then a valuable ring disappeared. We found it some time later, lodged in the carpet in the bathroom. I couldn't understand how it came to be there and how we had missed seeing it before.

One day when a plumber was working in the house I noticed an old clay pipe on a bedroom window sill and asked him if he had left it there. He replied no. When I went to fetch the pipe it had disappeared.

I spent the days before Christmas putting up decorations and brought in some greenery from the garden but did without holly as I could find none with berries on it. My partner returned from work and went upstairs to change. Later he remarked on how pretty I had made the bedroom with the holly. I said I hadn't decorated the bedroom but when I went upstairs I was shocked to see that there was indeed holly – profuse with berries – placed over the pictures on the walls.

No resident had ever stayed long in the house. After two years we decided to move on, not because we were worried by the strange happenings, but because we needed more room. The day we made this decision a securely fixed picture fell off the wall, leaving the picture hook intact.

We had fun and games when we put the house on the market. Sometimes, while someone was looking round it, the cottage would glow and surfaces and windows would sparkle. The old beams seemed smooth, showing the patina of age, and the house would feel warm, comfortable and spacious. At other times, even on a sunny day, the rooms appeared dark and cramped and there would be a dank smell in the air. Cobwebs, which I knew our efficient cleaner couldn't have missed, appeared in dusty corners and the beams looked as if they had a bad attack of woodworm. The windows appeared grimy and smoky and sometimes a thin film of wood ash would materialise on the quarry tiling. At these times the viewers couldn't leave fast enough and I learned not to expect them to make an offer.

The cottage eventually picked its new occupant, a lovely, cheerful woman in her mid-fifties.

Neither my partner nor I ever considered ourselves to be psychic and we aren't given to flights of fancy.

Ann and visitors to the cottage never actually saw the ghost, but as well as visible signs such as objects disappearing, the house seemed to change in the way it was perceived, so that sometimes it felt dull and unwelcoming and at others bright and cheerful. Though the fireplaces were blocked up, friends smelled smoke in the sitting room, but Ann did not. We are all sensitive to different triggers.

Although few people may have such tangible evidence of a presence in their home, many of us automatically sense the presence of a ghost in a house. We may feel him or her as a cold spot, a room that is never warm even in summer or strange smells that seem unrelated – tobacco where no one smokes, baking bread or quite unpleasant odours if the phantom is unfriendly or unhappy.

Clairsentience is a natural way of receiving impressions and from my own research I have discovered that the sense of smell is a good way of developing psychic abilities of all kinds.

Some people pick up such scents from the past wherever they go, as Lisa's story demonstrates:

My husband and I recently bought and moved into a small, 50-year-old cottage in North Carolina. It does its share of creaking and groaning, but considering the building codes here 50 years ago, I do not attribute anything otherworldly to the noises.

However, about a month ago, my husband and I were getting dressed to go out. As I went back and forth between the bathroom and our bedroom, through the little hall, I began to notice an odd odour, as if something sweet was burning. I checked the kitchen but there was nothing burning. The fireplace had not been used in two weeks. I went back to the hallway. The smell was now very distinct – cherry-pipe tobacco.

I called my husband. He has always accused me of having super-smelling powers, and mocks the way I sniff out the source of odours, but on this occasion he came into the hallway and said, 'Whew! Who's been smoking a pipe?'

We checked all around our house. Not a soul was to be seen outside. The heat had been turned off for at least a half hour, and when I raised the thermostat to start the boiler to check for a smell, there was none. The scent disappeared after a short time, and we haven't smelled it since. I imagine that our 1945 cottage was built for a World War Two veteran who enjoyed a good pipe every now and then.

In Florence, Italy, about seven years ago, my husband and I stayed in a large building that contained eight separate *pensiones*. We settled into a beautiful but small fourth-floor room with a view of the mountains, some antique furniture and a sink in the corner. The bath and shower were down the hall. Two girls from Australia were in the room next to ours. One of the girls could speak fluent Italian.

That night, I went to the sink in the corner of the room to remove my contact lenses, and I could smell wax burning, the way churches smell when many candles are lit. I made my husband sniff the area but he did not smell a thing. The next morning, the smell was gone.

I asked the girls next door if they had been burning a candle but they had not. That night, I smelled the wax again. This time I asked the girls to come in to sniff. They smelled wax too. The girl who spoke Italian found the proprietor of the *pensione* and asked about the waxen smell.

He explained that the entire building had been a monastery for several hundred years, and that the fourth floor had been where the monks had their cells. In the corner of each room, they had had a prayer stool and candles so they could pray through the night. The proprietor said that the smell was 'in the walls', but I wondered why the wax could be smelled only at night, only in my room, and why didn't my husband smell it too? No monks ever appeared to me but I did smell the burning wax every evening we were there, after 10 p.m.

Using Scents as a Catalyst for ESP

Often a fragrance can breach the dimensions. If you stand near a bowl of dried lavender in an old house you can sometimes connect to people from other ages for whom such fragrant herbs were scattered in the rushes to keep away infection.

Visit a medieval kitchen in an old castle when there is a demonstration of bread-making or spit-roasting and you will sense the bustle of the kitchen, feel the intense discomfort as the young boy turning the meat tries to shield himself from the intense flames, link into the weariness of the scullery maid as she carries the heavy iron pots. You may hear voices and see flashes of colour or images.

Stand in an ancient herb garden and close your eyes. Fishbourne Roman Palace in West Sussex has a lovely reconstructed Roman herb garden. You can smell the aniseed sharpness of fennel whose seeds were chewed by Roman soldiers to give courage, the clean bite of rosemary that the armies and household used as antiseptic on wounds, the rich tang of purple flowering sage or *herba sacra* dedicated to Jupiter that acted as both sedative and to relieve chest complaints. The sights, sounds and above all the conflicting emotions of the Celtic tribal leader, who ruled on behalf of the Romans but must have chafed for his freedom and that of his people, will be carried on the cumulative fragrances.

In an industrial museum, on days when the exhibits are in steam, you can taste the oil and the heat of factories and mills and the rhythmic trancelike repetition of the workers' actions, surrounded constantly by noisy, relentless, greedy machines.

Inhale the rich roses in a formal Tudor garden and sense the love and hopes and maybe despair. When you visit old places carry with you such clairsentient transmitters as a tiny lavender sachet or a phial of pine oil. Or sit in the café, if it is in an old part of the house, and sniff freshly baked cakes.

If you want to evoke the presence of a deceased loved one, sprinkle a favourite perfume from the past on your pillow, rub your furniture with lavender polish or starch your linen. You will feel the love surrounding you, perhaps a light touch on your shoulder or a fleeting shadow, and recall the happiness you shared. You may continue to smell the fragrance long after it has naturally faded.

Anne lost her beloved daughter Sarah when she was only 16:

One of the first experiences I had was when I was in Sarah's bedroom about three weeks after her death. I had sprayed some of her favourite perfume on to her quilt cover on the bed and put my head on it, stroking the cover with my eyes closed so that I could visualise her by her smell. When I opened my eyes, her tall mirror in the corner of her room tipped forward so that I was the image in the mirror and then it tipped back to its normal position. I went over to the mirror and touched it, stamped on the floor, but I could not get it to tip forward or backward as it had done at that moment.

Mandy, who was separated from her mother as an infant and given up for adoption, described her uncanny sensations when she worked as a nurse:

> I used to feel strangely drawn to a house by the hospital when I jogged past it. It turned out to be the house where I was born. I also hated the nurses' home, a gloomy Gothic building, and could not settle there and eventually moved out. It was the building where my mother had convalesced when she could not keep me.

Clairsentience and Decision-Making

Clairsentience is not only an important skill for detecting ghosts. It can also serve as a warning against present dangers or potential hostility. The ability to sense that a stranger or recent acquaintance is untrustworthy, although his or her outer appearance or actions offer no apparent justification for this distrust, is in-built in us all, but too often we do not recognise or acknowledge this protective system.

Dogs growl at some strangers but not others, while a normally confident child backs away from a friendly smile and outstretched hand instinctively. In both cases the person usually proves unreliable or to have negative intentions behind the smile and soft words. 'He or she didn't smell right' is one expression used by children.

People say, 'I knew as soon as I walked through the door that the residents had had an argument.' ... 'My office colleagues were plotting behind my back.' ... 'The party or date was going to be a disaster.'

This sixth-sense awareness is our most valuable tool, not only as a warning but also to show us the people we can trust and situations that will be advantageous to us. We should harness this skill to discover whether someone is trust-worthy:

☆ If possible try to observe the person across the room so that you are not initially influenced by a voice or a hand-shake. You will register body-language clues, but some people are remarkably adept at masking intentions and feel-ings.

☆ Most importantly let all your senses absorb impressions when the person in question is saying something you know to be true. However good people may be at concealing their intentions and feelings on a surface level, there are always subtle changes when they consciously lie. Let your senses register these changes subconsciously as they slide from truth to falsehood.

☆ See your psychic antennae spreading outwards to enclose the person in question, as you still your mind from formulat-ing conscious impressions.

☆ You may experience a sensation in your stomach or find the hairs on the back of your neck standing up.

☆ Try to isolate and identify your own feelings towards the person: panic, unease, excitement, sexual attraction, danger, spiritual wisdom.

☆ Now read the signals he or she is giving off on this deeper level: secrecy (which is not the same as protection of privacy), possessiveness, unreliability, deviousness, open-ness, altruism, kindness.

☆ These early impressions are invariably accurate and form a good precursor to a good working relationship, friendship or love affair that comes from the heart but which sometimes lacks the clarity of this protective clairsentient radar.

☆ If someone feels untrustworthy, you may decide to follow your heart or conscious mind, fall in love, lend money or share your innermost secrets. But at least you have been fore-armed and so enter into any relationship of trust or friendship with open eyes.

If we can trust our clairsentient abilities and use them without preconceptions we may be pleasantly surprised that someone we dreaded meeting or anticipated feeling an instant dislike for is a kindred spirit.

Clairsentience and Places

Sometimes a house or place of work can feel wrong instinctively. The Chinese account for this by saying that the building has bad feng shui, perhaps because its previous owners suffered persistent bad health and misfortune, or because the main entrance is facing the wrong direction, or its staircase faces the front door so that positive energy or chi rushes straight out.

There are times when no amount of redecoration or rearrangement can lift the gloom. A house can have an unhappy atmosphere because of some past tragedy or because the present owners are generating hostility within their relationships. Then we may have to make the best of a new residence or place of work. The psychic protection rituals described in Chapter 2 can cleanse a home of negativity. If there is an option, it may be better not to have to live or work in a place that feels wrong.

EXERCISE: HOME-HUNTING

If you are not currently house-hunting, choose the home of an acquaintance or colleague that you have a chance to visit and test out the atmosphere.

Begin by looking at the outside of a house or apartment block. It may be brightly painted with neatly manicured lawns, but does it feel right for you? If you are reluctant to enter, you should take these feelings seriously.

Inside the front door, pause and let the sensations wash over you. Are the hall and stairs welcoming, or do they emit feelings of foreboding?

As you progress from room to room, note any cold spots or inexplicable shadows. Are there any smells that seem not to be associated with the present owners — smoke in one corner of a room with no fireplace in a non-smoking household, a strong fragrance of flowers in a particular spot where there are no blooms? Do they seem to follow you as you walk around the house?

This is especially significant if the people with you detect nothing. Comment if the smells are agreeable and the owner may be able to explain the source. If he or she seems puzzled or embarrassed, you may have uncovered a resident ghost, but if this feels friendly there is no problem.

If at any spot you suddenly feel tremendous grief or fear or that you have to leave, ask to see the garden and let the feeling subside. Return to the spot and discover if the impression returns but is linked only to one place or room.

If you have not done so already, go into the garden or

yard. Do you sense land where there was once conflict, or does it exude peace? Abbey closes have their fair share of monastic ghosts, but tend to give off peaceful vibrations.

Before you commit yourself to rent or buy a home, take your children (or ones you can borrow) as they are expert in clairsentience. Knock on the door on the pretext of having left a glove or a key. If the children do not comment, ask them casually what they thought of the house.

Walk your dog past and pause at the gate. Does he or she growl or try to rush past? Dogs, like children, are natural psychics.

If you have doubts but feel logically a property would be ideal, do a little detective work. Does the house or apartment change hands far more than a similar property in the same road? If the house is empty, enquire about the previous owner or owners.

Should there have been a recent divorce in the house, it may have a temporary but removable bad atmosphere that can be eliminated using one of the rituals listed in Chapter 2. However, if all the previous owners over the past 50 years got divorced, could there be a connection with the home?

If the previous owner died after many years in the home, you might have a ghost, but it will be a friendly one who may even do some tidying or rearrange the furniture.

If anything feels strange, go to a local history library or museum, and investigate the area. You may understand your feelings. You may not want to live on the site of a Victorian abattoir or workhouse, but might be happy with a street market, although you may get lively ghosts plying their wares.

Sometimes the unease can relate to a potential but carefully concealed problem. Your impressions may be alerting you to the fact that a new house is built on a landfill site or a very old mineshaft or that you may have trouble with subsidence and flooding – you may have experienced a sinking sensation in your stomach or feel suddenly cold or wet. If in doubt, check again until you are sure.

Usually, however, a new residence chooses us if we trust our innate clairsentient abilities. The moment we step through the front door of a prospective property we feel ourselves at home.

Of course you still need to look at potential visible problems such as woodworm, but if a house seems right, like slipping into a comfortable shoe, you can be sure of happiness there – and that any resident phantoms will be welcoming.

5

Clairvoyance

Clairvoyance which literally means 'clear seeing', is the ability to look beyond the normal world and describe people and events far away, perhaps in the future or even in other dimensions. It also describes the ability to see ghosts. The incident involving my son Jack, which I described in the Introduction, is a good example of clairvoyance. Somehow he knew that his father had fallen off his motorcycle but was all right, even though this was happening 40 miles away.

Throughout the ages certain people have been gifted with this ability, sometimes also known as second sight. One of the earliest recorded experiments in parapsychology was carried out to test this ability in 550 BC, when Croesus, King of Lydia, was eager to discover which of seven oracles had the most prophetic ability. He sent messengers to ask each of them simultaneously what he was doing at a certain hour. To make the test as hard as possible, he did the most improbable thing he could think of – he chopped up a tortoise and boiled it with lamb in a brass cauldron. The Oracle of Delphi was the only one to report the vision and smell of a tortoise and lamb cooking in a brass-lidded cauldron and so won the king's trust.

Remote Viewing

In America during the 1970s a great deal of research was conducted into 'remote viewing', the ability to describe events and places a long way off. The term 'remote viewing' was coined by Russell Targ and Harold Puthoff. After hundreds of experiments over ten years at Stanford Research Institute International in California, they concluded that remote viewing is a psychic experience that many people experience spontaneously. Even subjects who had little previous psychic experience could quite easily be taught to accurately describe buildings, geographical features, people and activities in locations at a distance removed. In some cases, greater accuracy was achieved when the location was removed even further from the subjects. People were also taught to see and describe the contents of opaque containers.

Here, as is often the case, psychic phenomena overlap. For some subjects in these experiments found they were most successful utilising a form of astral projection. When asked to look into a sealed room or at a distant place, they felt that their spirits actually left their bodies and travelled to the scenes which they later accurately described.

Astral Projection

Astral projection, also known as an out-of-body experience, is a state in which we dream or daydream of flying or floating and travel to places where we may meet deceased relatives, guardian angels, spirit guides or our own evolved self. Other experiences involve feeling ourselves rising above our body and seeing it sleeping or resting below.

Some people regard the astral self as a separate etheric or spirit body. Others believe that our mind has the ability to see beyond the confines of the body and out of the range of normal vision.

In some cultures the out-of-body experience is a normal aspect of sleep and among tribes as far apart as Greenland and New Guinea the soul is said to travel astrally during the night and the experiences are remembered quite vividly on waking. Shamans use drums, rattles, chanting and dance to promote altered states of consciousness where astral projection is induced.

Thinking in Pictures

I have found from my own research that spontaneous incidents of clairvoyance are triggered from the distant actions of people we know well; for example, you may have a vivid image, rather than just a feeling, of a child or partner at a time when he or she is under stress or in danger in a strange place. But waiting for our loved ones to be in danger is certainly not a satisfactory way to practise clairvoyance. A far better and more relaxing way is to develop our ability to think in pictures.

As I mentioned in Chapter 1, modern people have neglected the ability to think in pictures. It is an ability that still exists for as children we gazed into the fire and saw pictures in the glowing coals and made up stories round them. It was well known to our ancestors. For untold centuries, men and women have gazed into pools lit by the full moon, seeking inspiration in images on the rippling water. Sometimes they have had clear visions of the future or events far away. From this practice, the art of scrying developed.

Scrying

Scrying, or looking into an object or substance with a reflective surface to capture clairvoyant or psychic images, has been practised from the earliest times, rather like holding an idea in a bubble or laying out your dreams. The term comes from the English word 'descry', which means 'to make out dimly'.

The practice, sometimes pronounced 'shreeing', was developed in Ancient Egypt, the Middle East, China, Greece, Rome and throughout Europe. It continued in an unbroken tradition for thousands of years. Though we think of clairvoyance mainly in terms of mysterious fortune-tellers prophesying as they turn their cards, gaze into crystal spheres or read our palms, the most important and widespread clairvoyant practice comes from the folk tradition of scrying.

This ability to recognise and project images from the deepest level of wisdom, whether we define this as our own or as the collective wisdom of mankind, as the psychologist Carl Gustav Jung called it, is the heart of all scrying. You can use the images in a tea cup, shadows on the wall made by a candle or a sudden, sharply focused picture that appears in your mind as you are carrying out repetitive tasks such as digging the garden or peeling potatoes.

From the beginning of civilisation, as women washed clothes at the family washtub or in a river, they would see images in the suds, lulled by the rhythmic, repetitive action (see page 16). Another domestic art is the tea-leaf reading that many of our grandmothers practised, dispensing intuitive wisdom along with common sense around the kitchen table. Lovers and mothers with sick children would gaze into the candle flame, the former calling a partner to respond to desire focused on the flickering flame, the mother watching pictures form in that state of combined exhaustion and vigilance. The common element is the semi-hypnotic state of stillness of body and mind in which the inner eye can express its visions. This can be acquired through meditation and breathing, but also by natural physical actions. Our grandmothers saw many a vision in the shining surfaces of furniture they lovingly waxed with lavender polish, long before essential oils were commonly used to invoke psychic awareness. These homely forms of divination are equally as powerful as the finest crystal ball. Because they are rooted in ordinary lives they are safe and gentle ways of accessing unconscious wisdom.

Scrying with Water and Inks

The easiest form of scrying if you are new to the art involves the use of inks or dark oils, such as oil paint or a dark bath oil, floated on the surface of water to create an image. Most effective are either calligraphy inks or permanent ink cartridges that can be obtained in a wide range of colours. As you drop the ink into the water, it will swirl to make a picture or patterns.

Recently I have discovered, from my own work and from teaching people to scry in water and to use the crystal ball, that other psychic faculties are triggered by clairvoyant imaging, especially clairsentience. Some people experience feelings as though they were experiencing the projected image. For example, one client described being under the sea on a moonlit night, but feeling no fear, only a tremendous calm and then experiencing elation as the imagery changed to a clear white sky and herself soaring through it.

If you are reading for someone else, ask what they see and feel about an image that has been created. Make this a vital stage in your own clairvoyant imaging. You may even find that clairvoyant images evoke sounds in your mind's ear. Clairvoyance is at the centre of a honeycomb of overlapping psychic abilities.

Single-Image Readings With Ink and Water

Use a clear glass or wide, deep white ceramic bowl. Plastic is not so good as it absorbs the ink and may stain. Metal – for example, a silver rose bowl – works best with plain water and a candle.

Dropping ink into a silver bowl

☆ Ask a question or concentrate on an issue as you hold the container of water between your hands.

☆ If you are reading for someone else, ask the person to hold the container as they focus on the issue.

☆ Squeeze the ink cartridge or oil paint directly into the

water drop by drop. Alternatively, you can use a brush or dropper and add the inks one or two drops at a time. The person for whom the reading is intended should carry this out.

☆ Red, blue and black inks and paints give the clearest readings. You can use more than one colour at a time.

☆ Let the inks swirl on the surface to create an image.

☆ Scribble down a brief note of what the image evokes in you. Do not rationalise this image. The first idea that springs into your mind, no matter how unlikely, is usually the most accurate.

☆ If you are using this method for a friend, ask him or her what the image means. We all have our own unique image systems. Any good psychic reading is not a guessing game, but the coming together of two psyches for a purpose, i.e. to answer a question.

☆ You may see a whole picture rather than a single image.

☆ Note any feelings the image evokes, as well as related sounds or words. Occasionally people will hear a message from their unconscious wisdom or maybe the evolved or higher self or even guardian angel. This may indicate the first spontaneous stirrings of clairaudient abilities.

In *The Complete Guide to Psychic Development*, I describe using this method to obtain three images and a more detailed picture. In practice, this single-image technique is very effective, especially if you are not an experienced scryer or if you want an answer to a particular issue rather than a wider life view.

☆ If you want to add to the picture, or if the first reading seems not to answer the question, tip away the water, wash out the bowl and create a second or even third image. Put the three together as you would a three-card Tarot reading.

AN INK AND WATER READING

Kate had been made redundant from her post as a clinical psychologist and could only find a temporary one-day-a-week contract. Although with difficulty she could manage financially for a year with her redundancy money, Kate felt very angry and had suffered a great loss in confidence in her own abilities, even though the decision had been made on budgetary criteria at a higher administrative level and was not related to her performance. Her question was not focused, but Kate knew that she needed a new direction.

She dropped black ink into the water. The image in the ink, looked, she said, like a butterfly flying through a summer pine forest which was backed by tall mountains with ice caps even in summer. I mentioned that the butterfly was an ancient symbol of rebirth and regeneration and asked if a pine forest in the mountains meant anything to her. Kate told me that recently she had been aware of butterflies everywhere, although it was only early summer. Unusually several had come into her top-floor flat. But Kate was far from a new beginning.

I suggested that she concentrate on her feelings about the image. She said that she felt as if a breeze was blowing her and the butterfly, which were maybe one and the same, through the pine forest and that she could taste

pure air and pine needles. She could hear children laughing and calling and this sound excited her, as though she
was creating the happiness.

Could there be a connection between her future and
children, though I was unsure about the pines and mountains. A holiday, perhaps?

Kate instantly understood. She had seen a job advert-
ised in a school in Canada, pioneering a new treatment
for autistic children that might help them to communicate
with other people more freely. Because the post was
overseas, she had hesitated in applying, as uprooting
herself would be a huge step and the salary was quite
small, although her living expenses would be low as she
would live at the school. The picture seemed to be
suggesting that this course would be a right one. Kate
applied for the job, and moved to her school set among
the mountains and forests.

Kate understood the image far more clearly than I did.

Candle and Mirror Scrying

Candle and mirror scrying differs from ink and water scrying
in that the image is seen within the mirror, rather than
moving across the surface. However there are many ways of
evoking visions within a mirror using reflections and shadows
that are not, as some people think, distractions but the stuff
of which the psychic imagery is formed.

In many cultures and different ages mirrors have been used
for scrying. The mother of mirror scrying is Hathor, the
Ancient Egyptian goddess of love, music and dancing, who
was once entrusted with the sacred eye of Ra, the sun god,
through which she could see all things. Hathor carried a
shield that could reflect back all things in their true light.
From this shield she fashioned the first magic mirror. One

side was endowed with the power of Ra's eye to see every-thing, no matter how distant in miles or how far into the future. The other side showed the gazer in his or her true light, and only a brave person could look at it without flinch-ing.

Divination using candles and mirrors is especially effective for matters concerning love or family relationships or any people-related issues at work.

You can conduct this form of scrying for yourself or with a partner or lover where the question is a joint one. It is espe-cially potent if carried out during the period of the Full Moon if you angle your mirror to reflect moonbeams, but it can be used at any time during the hours of darkness.

Use genuine beeswax candles, if possible, as these release a gentle scent of honey and are the original scrying candles. Beeswax tapers and eventually candles of undyed yellow were used for scrying and other rituals from pre-Christian times onwards, as bees were regarded as messengers of the gods and goddesses, so beeswax candles formed a link between mortals and the heavens. If you cannot obtain beeswax, candles dyed gentle purple or pink or pale yellow seem to work well. A variety of shapes and sizes can create different light intensities and levels.

☆ You can use either a large mirror (if you are reading for yourself and a partner), a mirror with a handle or a smaller mirror on a stand. The mirror should be oval and slightly convex. If it is a small mirror you may wish to use it only for divinatory purposes and keep it covered when you are not scrying.

☆ Work in candlelight or candle and moonlight.

☆ Place candles in a semi-circle at a safe distance behind you, so that the room is in shadow and the mirror reflects only your face (or that of you and a partner if the question is a joint one concerning your relationship).

☆ Arrange the candles so you can see shafts of light interspersed with shadows. Shadows may be cast by other objects in the room. Experiment so that the effect becomes slightly other-wordly in order to overcome conscious blocks in your mind.

☆ Sit so that you are at the side of the mirror and cannot see a reflection of your face. Move your position until it feels right. A partner can sit on the opposite side so that they can see in the mirror and maintain a counter-balance to your view.

☆ If you have any clear quartz crystals, set them to catch the candlelight, and you may get tiny rainbows appearing in the glass.

☆ Burn the incense or oil of sandalwood or frankincense for divinatory powers. Half close your eyes.

☆ Practise the visualisation breathing techniques described in Chapter 1; as you breathe gently in and out, visualise yourself absorbing the gentle golden light and exhaling all the jagged blacks, browns and greys, or dull reds of the day's frustrations and tensions.

☆ When you are relaxed, ask a question very softly out loud. Repeat it as a gentle mantra nine times, softer and softer until your voice is no more than a breath and the last one is spoken in your head.

☆ If you are working with a partner, ask the question alternately, so that one voice rises as the other fades.

☆ You may see the images either in the mirror or in your mind's eye, in which case you can cast the image on one of the light beams created by the candles into the mirror where it may change shape. As with water and ink scrying, you may picture whole scenes or landscapes.

☆ Half close your eyes and look first into the top right corner. This will tell you about the past.

☆ You and a partner may see different images, as you are literally as well as symbolically viewing the situation from different perspectives. Use them both to see a joint path and the reasons for the present situation or dilemma that may be rooted in your separate pasts.

☆ Close your eyes for a moment. Open them again and focus on the centre of the mirror to see the present issue.

☆ Close your eyes again. As you open them, look into the far top left of the mirror and see what is coming into your life.

☆ You can carry out candle and mirror readings for a friend about an issue in their life. Follow the same procedure as for a joint reading but, as it is not your question, ask the person what he or she sees in the mirror or the picture evoked in the mind's eye. Most people respond instantly and you should only offer your own images or interpretation if the other person is struggling. Even then, gentle questioning and inquiries about the feelings evoked by the image will usually provide the correct meaning.

☆ Afterwards rub the mirror gently with dark silk to cleanse it, moving in anti-clockwise circles.

☆ Wash out the silk gently under cool running water, and leave to dry naturally.

What do the Images Mean?

The images will, if you allow them, suggest relevance to the question you asked. We all have personal image systems, built up from childhood and modified over the years. For one person a dog might represent a loyal friend. For another it might be a terrifying attacker, depending on their experience of dogs. A symbol system is never fixed but most people's do have common factors based on what Jung called archetypes, meanings that have held true in many times and places: the wise man or woman, the messenger, the young hero or fool often identified with the self, the Sun and the Moon.

Use the symbols provided on pages 131–9 as a guide, changing any that are not right for you and adding to the list in your personal psychic development journal. Your own unique system will always be right for you.

Ghosts

The ability to see people from other dimensions is the one most associated with clairvoyance. Children do this quite spontaneously. Often the old man or woman they see in their bedroom was a former resident who was happy in their former home and remains there or perhaps pops back occasionally to check up on the beloved house, much as some ghosts visit relatives at the time of a wedding or birth in the family.

Sue's story is a perfect example of the type of ghost encounter experienced by adults as well as children – if we trust our natural psychic abilities:

We moved into a three-bedroom flat in Manchester when I was eight. After a week or two, I started seeing a little old lady sitting on the end of my bed knitting. The clicking of her needles woke me and she was quite solid and three-dimensional. She told me that I would really like the area, that there was a nice school just down the road and that I would soon settle.

She had a lovely, gentle face, and wore an old grey shawl, a white blouse and long skirt, and she was always knitting. My sister never woke up. I was not at all afraid as the old lady was so kind, but I told my mother about the old lady and she mentioned it to a neighbour. The neighbour asked me to describe the ghost and she said, 'Oh, that was the old lady who used to live there and died in the flat. She loved children.'

When I was settled in school after two or three weeks, the old lady stopped coming. Although I am in my forties, I have never forgotten her.

If you want to see ghosts, you need to link into their paths, the places where they walked or sat and looked out over a particular view. The following techniques work well for me, although you may see ghosts in your mind's eye or sense their presence, rather than seeing them as an external apparition. All the psychic senses converge and it is often the case that people begin with clairsentience and clairvoyance follows naturally.

In May 1998, as part of a programme for GMTV, I visited Charlton House, a Jacobean mansion designed by Inigo Jones which is now a community centre. The most prominent owner was Sir William Langhorn, formerly Governor of Madras, who had two wives but no heir and this was his great sorrow. His ghost has been sighted several times. The most spectacular results came during a pre-recording visit and were witnessed by a GMTV researcher. She saw curtains billowing although all the windows and doors were closed.

I first used a pendulum to trace the ghost path. I walked around the Long Gallery, where Sir William had been most frequently sighted and the pendulum began to swing strongly as I paced up and down a particular path opposite the fire-place. Here I linked into a strong feeling of Sir William's frustration as he raged at having no one to carry on his name. I later discovered it was at this spot that a woman saw lights in the Long Gallery and went to switch them off. But, she said, an invisible barrier stopping her moving any further.

At this point, the pendulum was moving in circles and although the windows and doors were closed, the curtains began to blow wildly. I saw Sir William with my inner rather than external vision, and was overwhelmed by his feelings. We did not stay any longer. If a ghost does not want you around, any polite visitor should leave with thanks.

To See a Ghost

Choose an unfamiliar place. Do not research its history.

☆ When you enter a stately home or even a ruined castle, ask if the ghost would mind you looking round. You need not say this out loud, but it is a courtesy when you enter someone's home, even if they died centuries before. Making a friendly relationship with a phantom is important. Ghost-hunters and ghost-busters are no more welcome to ghostly owners than insensitive visitors are to living ones who arrive unannounced and start poking around your private possessions.

☆ Try to build up a picture of your phantom by finding a spot in a room – a window seat where they might have often sat, a fireplace where the ghost might have stood for warmth in the winter, an arbour in a rose garden. As you pause here, see the view through the eyes of the ghost. This is the single most important step to clairvoyance of the past.

☆ If you have the chance to be alone – or if you have a domestic ghost who seems to inhabit a particular corner of a room – light a candle or shine a torch into the darkness and switch it off quickly. In the after-image you may catch a glimpse of the apparition.

☆ Use all your psychic senses: psychometry, to touch an old artefact and pick up impressions; clairsentience, perhaps using a lavender bag of your own or standing near a bowl of pot-pourri. You may connect with the ghost, who would have used similar fragrances to sweeten the air. You may be rewarded with a faint shadow, a flash of colour or even a full-blown vision. Rose perfume is popular with young female phantoms.

☆ Sense any cold spots, said to be located at the position where the air of two dimensions meets. Here again you may catch a faint shadow or a sighting. These cold spots are consistent in a room or building, no matter how warm the day. They often indicate a place where the ghost customarily sat or stood.

☆ When you have seen your ghost – and inner clairvoyance using the mind's eye can be just as accurate as any other – remember to thank the ghost. Do not take anything away from the house, not even a piece of loose fireplace, as you may disturb the natural vibrations.

☆ If you saw nothing, do not be disappointed. Ghosts are people and they may not have wanted to appear, just as some days you might not feel like answering the door or phone. Few people sense nothing and your clairsentient powers may be the first to operate.

☆ Read what you can about the house. Return again at a quiet time, armed with knowledge of the life and events that make up the history of the place.

☆ See if there is a ghost with whom you have a natural link. For example, you may both be mothers, like horses or be the youngest children in your families.

☆ The first time it is best to pick up clairvoyant impressions without the preconceptions of foreknowledge, but if you return on further occasions you will tune into the natural rhythms of the house and hopefully be rewarded with a glimpse of an earlier resident who in time will come to accept you.

EXERCISE: REMOTE VIEWING

Ask a friend or relation who is staying or holidaying in a place unfamiliar to you to concentrate at a fixed time for about a minute on a distinctive scene or unusual feature they can see and to photograph it. Remembering the test of King Croesus, ask them to avoid any obvious, routine action in order to eliminate any guess-work.

☆ Stop whatever you are doing for five minutes before the appointed time. Sit quietly, not consciously thinking of the person, but letting images form.

☆ Draw a sketch of salient features rather than using words, which can interfere with the spontaneity (you can write brief notes afterwards if you wish). Some people see the picture before the other person experiences it; as with telepathy experiments, some people naturally predict future events rather than pick up on the present, so note the time of any visions.

☆ Visualise the scene as though you were looking at a snapshot. You may find other psychic senses are triggered, so that you may smell flowers or cooking, hear church bells or a road drill or taste the salt of the sea or spices.

☆ Ask the sender to jot down any unusual aspects, sounds or fragrances, so that you can compare notes when you meet.

☆ When you see the actual photograph, you may sense a sudden feeling of déjà vu or describe aspects not recorded on the picture.

EXERCISE: REMOTE PREDICTIONS

When you have practised remote viewing and feel confi-dent, try scrying into the future. If you are visiting a new unfamiliar town or even a building, whether the house of a new acquaintance or an office, sit quietly at the exact time you will be there the next day and pick out a distinctive or unusual feature – a specific painting or ornament in a room, or an unusually shaped tower or building in the centre of a town. Home in on it from afar and bring your inner vision closer so that it fills your mind.

☆ Try not to rationalise or guess.

☆ Sketch rather than write your general impressions to keep your visual faculties to the fore, as these are a direct route to the psyche.

☆ If you practise this regularly, you will find you can tune into *routes* in advance. In time you will pick up potential hazards on your automatic radar if you remote view before a long journey. Again concentrate on unexpected hazards, rather than known bottle-necks.

EXERCISE: THE OBJECT IN THE BOX

☆ Ask a friend to place an unusual household or garden object in a box.

☆ Half close your eyes and *see* the outline in your mind's eye.

☆ Draw the object rather than use words.

☆ Repeat the test over a period of time and keep a journal detailing your results. Look out for any anomalies like guessing the contents of a later box.

Children are brilliant at guessing the colours in a tube of

sweets or the numbers that will turn up on a dice, but this tends to be spontaneous. If you ask them to perform, they become anxious and block their natural abilities. Similarly, the last time we holidayed in Spain I amazed my husband and children by telling them the colour of our hire car. They were convinced it would be white, like the previous holidays, but because I was so excited about the prospect of touring in it, I had a sudden vision of a red car – which it was. But try me with a card-guessing test and I am so bored by the prospect that any intuition dries up immediately.

You may also find that guessing the contents of boxes also lacks any emotional involvement. If this is not for you, concentrate on scrying for real hazards instead and use divinatory scrying to answer real-life questions and dilemmas.

6

Clairaudience

Who has not heard voices in the wind, the leaves rustling through an oak grove? That we talk of a stream chattering over stones is no mere figure of speech, for all natural sounds have voices that answer our deepest, sometimes unvoiced questions. The Native Americans listen to the wisdom of the stones, the birds, the animals and the trees. European myths tell us that there were once talking animals, birds and trees in woodlands and fields whose knowledge offered a guide. Now we no longer hear them because we no longer trust our power of clairaudience. But we can, with practice, rediscover our inner ear.

Clairaudience is primarily the ability to hear words or sounds that are not part of the material world. These sounds can, like clairvoyant visions or psychometric impressions, give access to understanding deep within us and, some people believe, beyond ourselves, in our higher evolved selves or with guardian angels or spirit guides.

Just as clairvoyance is channelled through the visual imaging powers that have been replaced by the more limiting written word, so clairaudience uses not only words, but animal and bird sounds, music and natural whisperings of foliage, the peal of church bells, the sound of drums, crashing waves and the hiss of steam to convey meanings and feelings. The majority of clairaudient experiences occur spontaneously.

Dr Ikechukwu Azuonye, a consultant psychiatrist, reported in the *British Medical Journal* in 1998 that a woman was saved from a potentially fatal brain tumour after voices inside her head told her to return from holiday abroad and to go to the brain-scan department of a major hospital, a place that few people had heard of. The patient had no outward symptoms of a tumour and could not have known that she had one. Dr Azuonye commented:

> As she arrived, the voices told her to go in and ask to have a brain scan for two reasons – she had a tumour in her brain and her brain stem was inflamed. The voices told her that they used to work at Great Ormond Street Hospital in London, but they did not say who they were or whether they were living or dead.
>
> However, neurosurgeons discovered a large tumour and were able to save her life by operating immediately. A tumour that size pushes the brain down and death comes within minutes if it is not treated. This is the one and only case I have come across of its kind.
>
> As she regained consciousness after the operation she heard the voices saying: 'We are pleased to have helped you, goodbye.'
>
> The patient made a full recovery and enjoys good health.

Ghostly or discarnate voices are usually heard because a person's auditory channels are tuned to this extrasensory wavelength and are linked solely to the person who hears the message rather than attached to a location. This personalised voice may be that of a deceased relative, a warning voice from another dimension, perhaps that of a guardian angel or our own inner voice that can instinctively lead us on to the right path. The concept of being guided by disembodied voices can seem worrying, especially as certain mental illnesses are characterised by voices suggesting bizarre or dangerous choices.

The true inner voice is heard only at important times and offers advice that we instinctively know is a guide to right action. As with the case above, the voices can even be a life-saver. Such experiences are not uncommon, although usually the voice is one familiar to the recipient of the message, especially where the message is urgent:

One morning Alison, who was 30, was alone in the exercise yard of her local riding school. A sudden sound caused her horse to panic. He knocked her to the ground and reared over her. Then Alison heard her grandmother who had been dead for five years say: 'Roll towards my voice, Ally.'

Alison was stunned and didn't respond. The voice became more and more insistent until she moved towards her dead grandma's voice at the moment the hooves came crashing towards her head. The horse caught only the edge of her chin and she escaped with lacerations.

Echoes From the Past

Voices or footsteps from the past may also be heard in old buildings, historical sites or battlefields where strong vocal imprints from previous occupants remain. These sounds across the ages may be triggered by the slightest stimulus. Several people may independently hear the voices or ghostly sounds. Sometimes even a new building on the site of an old hospital or prison can retain the sounds of former residents. Certain houses retain the footsteps of former owners who may have crossed a landing year after year to tend to a sick relation. The ghost may talk to the family and, if he or she likes them, watch over them. Caroline told me:

We lived in an old cottage close to Anne Hathaway's cottage near Stratford-on-Avon. One morning I was in bed when I heard someone say in a country accent, 'Good morning.' It was an old lady's voice. My husband was downstairs in the bathroom but I thought he was being stupid – until I heard the water running.

A cousin of mine came to stay and heard an old lady's voice say, 'Good morning, Stuart.' We hadn't mentioned the old lady to him.

In the middle of one night, my husband suddenly leaped out of bed and dashed downstairs. It was cold as we had no central heating. Soon he came back.

'You were right,' he said.

'What do you mean?' I asked as I had not said anything.

'You told me a log had fallen out of the fire on to the mat and you were right. It was lucky I went down at that moment as it was smouldering.'

I had not spoken. It must have been the old lady. The cottage was thatched and there was only a small window in the bedroom. We could not have escaped in a fire.

Developing Clairaudient Abilities in Old Places

Ancient sites — whether stone circles, an industrial museum or a meticulously restored stately home — are perhaps the easiest settings in which to rediscover the clairaudient abilities of childhood. Many people have reported hearing church bells at the side of lakes, only to learn later of legends of sunken villages beneath the water.

☆ Choose a place in which you feel at home, perhaps one you have visited before. Unlike clairsentient or clairvoyant experiences, clairaudient voices are not so easily verifiable by studying the history of the site, so foreknowledge may help you to tune into the sounds of past times.

☆ It may, however, be possible afterwards to understand the context of a seemingly unrelated sound by detective work in a local museum or library. For example, in Cornwall on Bodmin Moor where there are disused tin mines, echoes of this once thriving industry can be heard on misty evenings and at dawn at times when shifts would have started or ended.

☆ Visit your chosen destination early or late in the day or season, on a misty day if possible when earthly sounds are muffled.

☆ Unlike clairsentience, clairaudience works best if your body is moving rhythmically to a regular background sound: a ride in a horse and cart around the grounds or an ancient forest, a steam train or tram in an industrial museum, the hiss of steam of exhibits in a Victorian science collection, the lowing of cattle on a medieval farm. You could wear boots and splash through puddles at a standing stone in winter, crunch through autumn leaves or crisp snow. Wander through a water garden with splashing fountains.

☆ Try a museum of fairground organs, a collection of old instruments, even battle or air-raid noises in a regimental museum.

☆ Concentrate only on the background sound. Exclude all other thoughts, and look straight ahead. Gradually any distracting murmur of voices, birdsong or intermittent laughter will merge into a single voice, perhaps one you recognise from dreams or your childhood, snatches of song unrelated to the context, sudden cannon fire or a peal of bells. You may hear a single word, a phrase or a message come into your head. Do not try to analyse it or to question how such words or sounds could relate to the present setting.

☆ Your clairaudience may be accompanied by images, smells or impressions. You may get several sounds and messages, or a single one.

☆ When you feel the world intruding once more, or you are tired, stop. Sit quietly and record in your journal the words and any associated impressions, your feelings and the context.

☆ As you practise, you will find that you begin to pick up sounds and voices during early morning or evening walks, even around urban streets as you tune into vocal impressions of past ages. Market Street and Abbey Way may now be filled with supermarkets or high-rise apartments, but they retain their earlier street cries or monastic chants. The most mundane sounds – the whirr of a sewing machine or the hum of a vacuum cleaner – can provide the backdrop for clairaudient messages and other-age, as well as other-worldly, sounds.

☆ In time your inner voice will get stronger, advising and warning you of hazards and opportunities. This urgent prompting is very different from free-floating 'what-ifs'. Some people go on to channel messages from their higher or evolved self or angelic guides. Only if the inner world intrudes too frequently on the outer – and this is true of all psychic work – should you take a break and concentrate for a time on physical work and mundane tasks to restore the balance.

Clairaudience in Nature

I began the chapter by talking about natural sounds, the wind in the trees and water chattering over stones. The prophets and prophetesses of old did use elaborate tools for divination, but they tapped their clairaudient abilities to hear what they regarded as the natural voices of the deities and nature spirits. Water is a natural oracular medium, whether in the form of sacred springs or the flow of the sea on a shingle shore, in what T.S. Eliot called 'the silence between two waves'. Or the roar of a waterfall that blocks out all other earthly sounds, a gentle domestic water feature or even a fish tank aerated by a gurgling pump in your living room or work area.

At Dodona, the ancient oak grove and sanctuary of Zeus situated near Epirus, the oracular priestesses would put their ears to the ground to receive answers, murmured so low they could be heard only in the mind. The priestesses also interpreted the sounds of leaves rustling through the oak groves or water under rocks, not only for inspiration on the state affairs of great kings, but also on the issues of love, happiness and health that still form the touchstone of everyone's lives today.

Talking Stones

Talking stones have a very ancient magical tradition. If you can find a natural source of water where it flows over pebbles, you can listen to the wisdom formed by the fusion of stone and water. An urban stream or tiny fountain in a city square can be as potent as listening to the ocean crashing on jagged rocks, if less dramatic. Whatever the source of the water, ask a question or focus on an issue and listen to the answer, which may come as a stream of words or a single word or phrase.

You can also use rain falling into a bowl of stones. Rain water is said to have healing properties when it fell on Ascension Day or any time during June. However at any time rain water offers a profound medium for talking stones. The water must fall directly into the bowl from the sky and not touch either a roof or leaves as it descends.

☆ Choose 20 or 30 small pebbles of different shapes and sizes from places with happy memories for you. These stones should come from or be near water, a shore, a river bank or a lake, preferably a natural rather than manmade setting.

☆ Keep them in spring water when not in use, in a glass or crystal bowl with an amethyst or rose quartz to energise them. Leave them in a place where they can absorb sun and moonlight freely.

☆ Use or create a source of running water from which you can easily retrieve your stones after asking your question(s). For example, you could use a garden fountain, a hose or cold tap run slowly into a large tin bath, plastic or metal bucket or a wooden water butt.

☆ Take a handful of stones from your container and cast them into the running water. As you do so ask or focus on a question. Let the question arise spontaneously. If there is nothing specific, let the stones talk to you about your hopes and dreams.

☆ Close your eyes and let the water form the sound of words or a single phrase.

☆ Do not stop to unravel the significance of the answer. If you have another question, pull out another handful of stones and cast these into the running water on top of the first.

☆ You can continue as long as you have stones to cast.

☆ Put together the separate answers. They may provide a coherent message or make up strands as in a story. If the message is not clear, sit with your eyes closed next to the running water and let any words, sounds or even images enter your mind.

☆ If you still are not clear, go for a walk or dig the garden – spend the rest of the day absorbed with practical tasks.

☆ When you have finished with your talking stones, sprinkle them lightly with sea salt to cleanse them of any negative thoughts, dry them gently and place them back in the glass container.

☆ At night, slip the paper with the words under your pillow. As you drift into sleep recreate the sound of the water on the stones or play a tape or CD of sea or river music (see page 145 for suggested sources). The connection will come in your dreams, which will probably involve water.

Naomi had collected her stones from the shores of a Scottish loch on her honeymoon, intending to make rune stones but she had never used them. Now, two years later, having just taken a new high-powered job on a woman's magazine she found herself unexpectedly pregnant. Naomi had lived with her husband for ten years before their marriage, but children were not on the agenda. Karl was delighted with the news, but Naomi, who was already feeling very nauseous, was upset as the other women in the office were young, single and very ambitious.

She cast her stones into the pebble pool in the garden and the small jet of water bubbled up to her unvoiced question 'How can I cope?'

'Be like the she-wolf,' the answer came, 'the strength is in the pack and the joy is in the suckling.'

Naomi understood instantly. Her great-grandmother, who was a very old lady when Naomi was born, used to read Rudyard Kipling's *The Jungle Book* to Naomi when she was a child, especially the stories of Mowgli who was suckled by the she-wolf. At that moment, Naomi felt her great-grandma near and could smell her favourite lavender water.

Naomi explained that her great-grandmother had a hard life as she was one of eight children. She struggled to learn to read at night school after her day at the factory. But the old lady always spoke of the joys of her childhood rather than the sorrows, and she held the family together until her death, mending any quarrels with the words Naomi had heard.

Naomi suddenly had a picture of how emotionally empty her own life had become. She and Karl often spent weeks apart, preoccupied with career matters. When the baby was born Naomi called her Ruth after her great-grandmother and decided to work from home, writing about issues concerning mothers and children.

Was Naomi's inner wisdom talking, or had her great-grandmother spoken to her through the water? The result was the same.

EXERCISE: TALKING TO THE TREES

This is another art practised in Zeus's oak grove at Dodona where there stood his sacred prophetic oak. Wood hewn from this tree acted as oracle to Jason and the Argonauts on their perilous journey in search of the Golden Fleece.

You need not use an oak grove, although the oak tree, symbol of strength and wisdom, was the divinatory tree of the Druids, as well as King of the Forest in classical tradition. Pine trees are symbolic of illumination, the ash of broad vision and endurance. Birches herald new beginnings, willows intuition and the rowan protection. The aspen, or white poplar, was called the shiver-tree because its leaves shake even when there is no breeze. You can therefore ask the aspen tree at any time and its answers will be tempered with healing, its salient property.

☆ Wait until a windy day. Pause for a moment in a grove of trees, letting the sound of the leaves flow through you.

☆ If you have no specific question, let the breeze-blown leaves share their wisdom. Since oaks can live for more than 1,000 years and yews for 2,000, they have seen many ages and many joys and sorrows. They are good teachers, especially when you need to get issues into perspective.

☆ If there are questions or issues, take a knife and carve the initials of each word of your question on a fallen twig or small leafless branch.

☆ Wait until the wind pauses and cast the twig as far as you can, upwards or horizontally towards a clearing. The wind will answer very shortly.

☆ Close your eyes and listen to the words made by the leaves as they rustle.

☆ When the message is finished, wait in case there are any more words you need to hear. Images may flash through your mind, fragrances, emotions or impressions. Many of the other psychic senses are close to clairaudience.

☆ Finally touch the tree trunk of the nearest tree lightly. Let its strength and healing still any disharmonious thoughts and renew your energy.

7

Telepathy

Telepathy is usually considered in terms of mind-reading or sending messages on a mental telephone, but the term is more far-reaching than that. We all use telepathy automatically without thinking – children mind-hop all the time. It is usually very strong between family members, not only twins, but mothers and children, brothers and sisters, lovers and partners. Developing this ability, so that we can use it when needed, is an important step in unfolding psychic powers.

Diane lives in Ventnor on the Isle of Wight. Her husband Brian was working as head chef on the ship the *Rina del Mare*, and one of his jobs was to watch the stores being loaded. Suddenly Brian collapsed and had to be carried off to the sick bay with agonising stomach pains. After four hours he was fine and returned to work. During the hours that Brian was in such pain, unknown to him Diane was at St Mary's Hospital in Newport on the Isle of Wight, having an emergency gall-bladder operation.

What is Telepathy?

Telepathy is defined as the transmission of ideas, thoughts, feelings and sensations from one person to another without words. The word telepathy comes from the Greek 'tele' (distant) and 'pathe' (occurrence or feeling) and was coined by Frederic W.H. Myers, a psychical researcher, poet and psychologist, who founded the Society of Psychical Research in 1884. A year later the American Society of Psychical Research was created and telepathy became the first psychic phenomenon to be studied scientifically. Testing telepathy under laboratory conditions has always proved difficult. In 1930 the American parapsychologist J.B. Rhine began extrasensory perception (ESP) tests at Duke University in North Carolina using playing cards and Zener or ESP cards on which five different shapes were printed. He had problems finding enough people to score significantly above chance in his card guessing experiments.

Testing children is even harder than adults. The only researcher to have had significant success was Ernesto Spinelli, working at Surrey University during the 1960s. His experiments were stimulating for the children, using coloured guessing boxes, puppets and thinking caps to capture wandering attention spans. He found that measurable telepathic ability declined with age. The best subjects were three-year-olds. Second best were children aged five to eight, and after that all the groups scored at chance level. The scores were best if two children were approximately paired by IQ. Dr Spinelli hypothesises that the child uses the same thinking processes for telepathy as for normal thought. Once their thoughts become internalised the ability to mind-hop decreases. So far no one has been able to replicate his results.

Most telepathic experiments with children fail either

because the child loses interest or because they feel under too much pressure to succeed. When the teenage Creery sisters were investigated by the Society of Psychical Research in 1888, they scored remarkably well at card guessing, but the results were discounted when they were found using secret signals during sessions when they were in the same room. However, the sisters had been very successful when separated. They said they had not used signals in their most successful experiments and resorted to them only when they could not get results because they were anxious to avoid upsetting the testers.

Recent experiments have been more encouraging. Psychic ability may be spread throughout the population, according to Dr Deborah Delanoy, a senior researcher at the University of Edinburgh's psychology department, Britain's leading research centre into the paranormal. 'It's like music. There would be Mozarts and people with virtually no ability. Most of us would be somewhere in-between.'

Other experiments around the world found evidence which appeared to show that people were aware of facts that they could not have known through normal perception. Subjects in experiments at Edinburgh University are blindfolded, placed in an easy chair and played a tape of white noise, formless sound like an untuned radio, that relaxes them and prepares them for the experiment. A sender in another room then tries to transmit to the volunteer target thoughts of images and sounds, while the experimenter monitors and compares the thought patterns of the two. By the law of averages, there should have been similarities in about a quarter of experiments, but the Edinburgh team had a figure nearer to one-third.

ESP *Cards*

You can try card-guessing experiments to test your telepathic bond with close friends or family members. It involves transmitting pictures telepathically. Visual imaging is at the basis of all visualisation and much clairvoyant work.

☆ Photocopy the ESP cards (see page 100), a variation of the original Zener cards, on to thin white card, so that you have five of each design.

☆ Create each design in plain black, so that there is only one variable, in this case shape.

☆ If you wish to try something different, you can alternatively use five astrological signs, or five colours. The only proviso for creating your own design is that each of the five is distinct from the others and easily named.

☆ You may find when you check your test results that while direct telepathic transmission is low, sometimes people consistently pick the next card to be dealt or even two cards ahead, a form of precognition or clairvoyance.

☆ Cut out the photocopied shapes to make a card pack of 25 cards, small enough to handle easily.

☆ The easiest way of recording results is to use a test sheet of the type shown on page 101. The Sender should circle the card he or she has selected in the appropriate section each time one is turned over.

☆ Later this can be checked against the guesses the Receiver marked on his or her card.

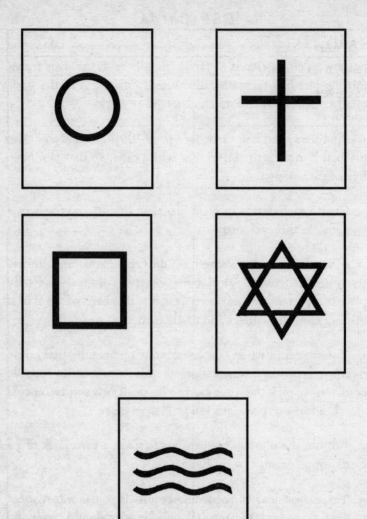

ESP cards: circle, cross, square, star and water

CARD TEST

Sender

Receiver   Date

Sender	Receiver
Circle Cross Square Star Water	Circle Cross Square Star Water
Circle Cross Square Star Water	Circle Cross Square Star Water
Circle Cross Square Star Water	Circle Cross Square Star Water
Circle Cross Square Star Water	Circle Cross Square Star Water
Circle Cross Square Star Water	Circle Cross Square Star Water
Circle Cross Square Star Water	Circle Cross Square Star Water
Circle Cross Square Star Water	Circle Cross Square Star Water
Circle Cross Square Star Water	Circle Cross Square Star Water
Circle Cross Square Star Water	Circle Cross Square Star Water
Circle Cross Square Star Water	Circle Cross Square Star Water
Circle Cross Square Star Water	Circle Cross Square Star Water
Circle Cross Square Star Water	Circle Cross Square Star Water
Circle Cross Square Star Water	Circle Cross Square Star Water
Circle Cross Square Star Water	Circle Cross Square Star Water
Circle Cross Square Star Water	Circle Cross Square Star Water
Circle Cross Square Star Water	Circle Cross Square Star Water
Circle Cross Square Star Water	Circle Cross Square Star Water
Circle Cross Square Star Water	Circle Cross Square Star Water
Circle Cross Square Star Water	Circle Cross Square Star Water
Circle Cross Square Star Water	Circle Cross Square Star Water
Circle Cross Square Star Water	Circle Cross Square Star Water
Circle Cross Square Star Water	Circle Cross Square Star Water
Circle Cross Square Star Water	Circle Cross Square Star Water
Circle Cross Square Star Water	Circle Cross Square Star Water
Circle Cross Square Star Water	Circle Cross Square Star Water
Circle Cross Square Star Water	Circle Cross Square Star Water

Test sheet

☆ Photocopy enough sheets to record ten runs at a time and have separate cards for Sender and Receiver.

The Test

☆ Sender and Receiver should both look at the five designs before the test and agree that they are using the same names for them.

☆ It can be useful to spend a few moments together before the test, quietly imprinting the designs on your joint consciousness.

☆ The Sender and Receiver should, if possible, be in adjoining rooms, or, if not, on the other side of the room, the Receiver facing away from the Sender, looking at a plain wall, so that he or she cannot pick up any unconscious signals or be distracted by other visual stimuli. Use screens if necessary.

☆ The Sender shuffles the cards.

☆ When the test begins, the Sender should turn over the cards in the order they appear and continue turning the cards one by one until each of the 25 has been turned over.

☆ The Sender can ring a bell or use a buzzer or say 'Ready' or 'Now' each time they turn over a new card.

☆ They should look at it, taking ten seconds to transmit the symbol, at the same time circling the symbol on the Test Card, before turning over the next one.

☆ It can be helpful for the Sender to envisage the symbol

travelling on a wave of light to the Receiver, and for the Receiver to also visualise this light symbol coming towards them.

☆ The Receiver circles each choice on the test sheet in the Receiver's column, trying not to rationalise the decision or guess but recording the first answer that comes to mind.

☆ Use a stopwatch. Keeping going fast is important to prevent logic intruding on the Receiver.

☆ It is vital that the Sender does not comment in any way, as the Receiver might, consciously or unconsciously, begin trying to use logic to work out the run of cards rather than intuition.

☆ Repeat the test after shuffling the cards again.

☆ After five runs, have a short break before changing over. The Sender will become the Receiver for the next five. Do not discuss or try to assess the success of guesses.

☆ Remember you are not testing individual psychic ability, but the link between you, so add the two runs together to give you the total of ten runs.

☆ When you have carried out the ten runs, add up the correct number of guesses overall regardless of who made them. See how it compares with the ratings of significant scores listed below.

Interpreting Statistics

You can try this with different family members and friends and see how your scores compare. However, any test situation is artificial and does not reflect the living telepathic link rooted in love and the instinctive unspoken call of one person to another. If you and your soulmate score less than chance, it does not mean your love is doomed, but that you are not test people and would do better to concentrate on developing telepathic abilities where they operate best, in the real world.

Statistical significance and probabilities are incredibly complex and beyond the scope of this book. If you are interested in statistical significance, I have suggested further reading on page 150. For real-life purposes, the basic 'above chance' criteria is more than adequate.

After one run of trying to guess the cards the Receiver has a 50/50 chance of getting five out of the 25 guesses correct. If you calculate the results overall, this chance result becomes less likely the more runs you do. Mathematical calculations assess that there is only a one in 20 chance of getting nine correct in any single run of cards. These odds are generally acceptable to scientists against scores being due to luck.

If you take a one in five per run as your baseline for chance results, you have a rough idea of how to know if you are using ESP. If you want to assess these odds more accurately, I have listed a sample of what are called the 'significant scores', above which ESP is almost certainly operating, even by strict scientific standards. If you are consistently scoring above one in five on tests, then I and many other informal psychic experimenters would be happy to accept that telepathy is implicated between Sender and Receiver.

Number of Runs of 25 Guesses	Chance Score	Significant Score
1	5	9
2	10	16
3	15	22
4	20	28
5	25	34
10	50	63

ESP scores

Telepathy in Everyday Life

As well as occurring in a crisis, telepathy is a routine non-verbal bond between either blood relations, partners or those closely linked by love or strong friendship. This every-day link of love can be used with absent friends or family members. It operates using the normal channel of love cited above, so needs no psychic protection apart from good intent. As with all psychic development, do not work if you are feeling negative or exhausted.

☆ Pre-arrange a time to send loving thoughts to a friend or absent family member when you will be undisturbed each evening or morning.

☆ When you first wake up or just before you go to sleep are both times when conscious barriers are at their lowest.

☆ You may find it helps to light a candle and sit for a few minutes seeing in your mind's eye the absent person smiling. Tell the person with whom you are communicating to also light a candle at the beginning of the previously agreed time of the psychic contact and to gaze into it, visualising you in your customary place, perhaps a favourite chair or seated at the kitchen table, somewhere you may have shared many conversations in the past.

☆ Say in your mind a few words of encouragement or appreciation. On the first occasion try to transmit the name of a place you have visited together, a mutual friend from the past or a private joke, anything that has personal significance for you both and do not share with others.

☆ Visualise the scene, the mutual friend or the setting in which you shared the joke, as telepathy works best through the visual channels.

☆ Write down the message you are sending, plus any impressions you receive in return, so that you do not forget. If you visualised a place in the message, scribble down a sketch of what you pictured. A cartoon will suffice.

☆ Leave the same gaps in a psychic conversation as you would in an external one.

☆ At the same time the absent person should be sitting quietly listening and focusing on your message and returning his or her feelings. It is important not to try to rationalise the place or name chosen and, if nothing comes, not to force it. This is a first attempt.

☆ He or she should write down any words or images received as well as any general impressions about your contact, especially ones to do with emotions.

☆ After five or ten minutes, blow out the candles, sending light and protection to the source of the telepathic sending. The absent person should do the same thing at the same time.

☆ The next night reverse roles, so that the other person sends the first message. If you find that you are both simultaneously sending and receiving, this is quite natural, as it would be with any non-psychic conversation. It shows that you are meshing together telepathically.

☆ Try to transmit at the same time each day for an unbroken period of ten days if possible, to establish the rhythm.

☆ When you communicate by phone do not mention the sessions, tempting though it is, until the agreed period is over.

☆ After ten days exchange copies of the telepathic messages with the other person. You may find that you have both linked in, not to the actual words, but to emotions that you or the other person had been experiencing prior to and during the contact, whether they had a headache or serious underlying concerns.

Julia, who was communicating with a friend Liz who lived about 100 miles away, was worried on the first night because she could not find her purse. She tried to convey the test word, which was Josh, the name of the big pottery cat her friend had given for her last birthday. Liz wrote down 'purse' on the first night.

Sarah, a businesswoman in her fifties, was sending the message on the fifth night when she had a sudden spasm of pain in her leg that would not go away. Because she felt uneasy, straight after the session she rang her daughter Maria, not intending to mention the experiment. Maria said, 'I'll be surprised if you got anything tonight. As I was sitting with my candle, the dog rushed in and knocked the big pine stool next to me at the kitchen table on to my leg. I nearly went through the roof. My leg is badly bruised.'

Continuing the Link

You may find that your initial telepathic session was very reassuring. If so you can use it as an ongoing link. If you conveyed only general positivity rather than any specific information, do not be disappointed. This is the first vital step and you should continue with another ten-day cycle of telepathic links.

☆ Spend a little longer on each ensuing ten nights and hold a symbol that is meaningful to both of you as sometimes visual links are more easily transmitted.

☆ Once you have established a psychic link, you may wish to have a single weekly session.

☆ Gradually introduce messages to each other, first on alternate sessions and then simultaneously.

☆ As you become more confident, exchange snippets of news by telepathy, especially those of significance to you both in a personal way.

☆ Check these periodically with each other. After only a few weeks you will be surprised at your success rate.

☆ Arrange telepathically times to phone each other.

☆ Do not consciously mention the time to the other and try to pick times when you would not usually be in contact. Before long you will find the phone is engaged on every occasion.

☆ When you are really confident, send messages at a time which is not pre-arranged. Note the time, place and message. Get the other person to do the same and compare notes. You may find the other person suddenly thought of you at the time you were messaging, even if the message did not get through as such.

Strengthening Family Links

Send telepathic messages of love and encouragement to children and partners during the day at times when you know they will be experiencing stress, or to teenagers or adults who are away from home and may be missing the familiar environment.

One Canadian mother would send messages of love to her toddler in the work crèche. Whenever she phoned to see how he was, the staff reported the little boy would come over to stand by the phone from the other side of the room. He did that only when his mother phoned and the time of contact varied. A teenager in Wiltshire would stand beneath his mother's window and wake her telepathically if he forgot his key. It always worked, although she was a heavy sleeper.

Once the telepathic channel is in operation, you can also use it to ask a partner or flatmate to bring home some bread or coffee. I know several married couples who swear by their psychic shopping list.

Equally if you are going to be late and cannot get in touch with your partner or a friend, communicate telepathically. When you are together, spend times silently talking in your minds and after a few minutes you will find that you can continue the conversation even if it had not been a topic you had previously mentioned.

This works also with pets, whom you can mentally stroke if you are going to be late home or if you have to leave them to go away on business or holiday.

When you have used these methods successfully for a few weeks, try the card experiments again for fun. Your scores may have improved, even in the test situation.

EXERCISE: KEEPING A PSYCHIC JOURNAL

As I said at the beginning of this chapter, many people have regular spontaneous telepathic connections. Often we do not record them, and it may be hard to recall months or years later what happened. Rita, an American mother who has ten children, keeps a journal of all the amazing synchronicities or meaningful coincidences that occur and, especially with her adopted children, help to confirm the link of love within the family.

☆ Keep a small notebook with you, so that you can chart those times your mother rings precisely as you pick up the phone to dial her, the occasions when a friend halfway across the world sends the same but highly unusual birthday card to another mutual friend, those tantalising instances when a child suddenly echoes an unspoken thought or memory of an incident that happened before he or she was born or brings you the item or food you were visualising at that precise moment or minutes before.

☆ Copy these entries into your main psychic journal. As your psychic powers open, these will increase and give you confidence to trust your intuitive wisdom in other aspects of your life.

8

Dreams and Psychic Awareness

'Let us learn to dream – and then we may perhaps find the truth' – Friedrich A. von Kekule, professor of chemistry in Ghent, Belgium, addressing a scientific convention, 1890.

Jenny's parents had been decorating her teenage brother's room. During the night, she had a dream in which two older dark-skinned women came to her. One she recognised as her dead grandmother. They told her to wake up quickly, as there was great danger. She woke and saw smoke pouring under the door. Her brother's mattress, which had been propped against a light, had started to smoulder. There were gas cylinders downstairs. Jenny woke her mother, who was able to phone the fire brigade just before the phone went dead.

Later, when the family were safe, Jenny's mother asked what had woken her and Jenny described the two women. The second was Jenny's other grandmother – who had died before she was born.

Few of us will have dreams with such a dramatic effect as Jenny's. Nevertheless the world of dreams seems to offer a level of awareness that is not bound by the confines of time and space, when the barriers of consciousness are lowered.

Because this is mainly an introductory book, it does not cover the more complex phenomenon of lucid dreaming (the ability to be aware you are dreaming and to change the dream). However, I have included a simple exercise to intro-duce the subject and enable you to try encouraging lucid dreaming yourself. There is a further reading section and list of useful contact addresses at the back of this book if you want to study this matter in more depth.

Creative dreaming, for solving dilemmas and finding inspi-rational ideas, is a basic but important psychic skill. To maximise this channel of communication, it is important to develop accurate dream recall, thereby accessing the rich information offered during sleep but too often forgotten in the light of day.

The symbols listed on pages 131–9 are found in dreams as well as scrying and divination.

Creative Dreaming

Frederick A. von Kekule was involved in research to discover the question of the structure of the benzene molecule without success. One evening he fell asleep in a chair and had a dream in which long rows of atoms began to twist them-selves into a snakelike formation. One of the snakes caught its own tail and began to spin round in a circle. Von Kekule woke and, using the closed ring model seen in his dream, revolutionised organic chemistry.

In 1789 Ernst Chladni saw in a dream in precise detail an unfamiliar musical instrument. He experimented with the blueprint revealed during sleep, and invented the euphonium, a mellow-sounding instrument similar to a tuba.

Whether such flashes of inspiration are interpreted as psychic intervention by a higher consciousness, or innate wisdom that had been working on a problem at a deep unconscious level, in both cases the vehicle of the dream offered the elusive answer.

The psychologist Carl Gustav Jung was convinced that we all have access to a collective pool of wisdom that draws on all cultures and times, called by some philosophers the Akashic Records. These records, it is said, can be accessed in the sleep state, during astral projection or in a state of deep meditation. Some people are convinced that each new civilisation rediscovers knowledge buried beneath the sands or the sea as older civilisations were eclipsed.

A Basic Technique for Creative Dreaming

This method, which can be used to answer a question or give information that is not accessible to the conscious mind, is best carried out immediately before going to sleep.

☆ Have a leisurely bath and add jasmine, mimosa or rose essential oils, traditionally oils of creative dreaming. Use no more than ten drops in all in a full bath of water.

☆ In the bedroom, light a candle of pink or soft lilac. Place this on a heatproof tray.

☆ Write down a question to which you need an answer, the name of an object you have lost or a dilemma that is troubling you.

☆ Use a dream pillow, filled with dried rose petals or a

mixture of lavender and hops, beneath your usual pillow.

☆ As you sit in the candlelight, read the question then burn it in the candle flame.

☆ Blow out the candle, repeating the question once more. Then drift into the lilac or pink clouds of the extinguished candlelight.

☆ You may not get a direct answer in your dream, but if you interpret the dream as a story, there will be clues and cues – and you may even be inspired to invent or write something new as a result.

☆ If you cannot see any connection, write out again the original question before you start the day, and let your pen write without conscious thought.

Developing Dream Recall

Some people naturally recall dreams in great detail; others forget them almost immediately on waking. It is possible for anyone to improve dream recall by keeping a dream diary or journal next to your bed and noting dreams as soon as you wake. If you follow this procedure over a period of weeks, you will be able to use dreams as a source of intuitive knowledge, for forward planning and as warnings of avoidable obstacles that have not been registered by the conscious mind.

☆ Keep a pen and pad next to your bed.

☆ If a particularly vivid dream wakes you, note down the

salient points. Do not wait until morning, as details can fade or get overlaid by other dreams.

☆ Some dream experts advise deliberately waking yourself with an alarm in the middle of the night, but this can create a pattern of sleep disturbance that is counter-productive to healthy sleep and a natural cycle of dreaming.

☆ Where possible, do not use alarm clocks or radio alarms to rouse you in the morning as they can interrupt the slow transition between sleep and waking. Go to bed sufficiently early that you wake naturally. It may be best to begin your dream journal at a weekend or during a holiday, when you are not pressed to wake at set times or rush about as soon as you awake.

☆ If possible, allow yourself time in the early morning to recollect and record your dreams before the demands of the day intrude.

☆ As you wake, sit quietly and let dream images form in the waking mind. Record each with a word, a phrase or a scribbled picture or diagram.

☆ Begin with the most recent dream. Let this lead you back like a thread through your nocturnal wanderings. If images do not come spontaneously do not force them, but let your mind in this transient stage lead you quite naturally.

☆ If you cannot recall the whole dream, write down a key word, a predominant and perhaps recurrent image, mood or emotion. Do not attempt to unravel the meaning at this stage.

☆ You may find it easier to keep a tape recorder by your bed and to switch it on either when you wake in the night or first thing in the morning. Traditionally the oral tradition is one that lends itself to spontaneity and prevents you from subconsciously editing the dream as you write.

☆ Experiment with different ways of recording, drawing, poetry, even clay models.

☆ Let the meaning of the dream unfold naturally during the day, perhaps over two or three days if it is a specially significant dream.

Predictive Dreams

Dramatic predictive dreams are always spontaneous. As your dream work develops, you may find that minor and entirely avoidable hazards emerge in dreams. Predictive dreams do not always herald inevitable disaster. With practice you will learn to distinguish between free-floating anxiety dreams, in which all manner of disasters occur, and those warning dreams that can alert us to information not registered by the conscious mind, such as a worn tyre on the car or the need to check up on the health of a loved one who may not have shown any outward symptoms of distress.

Predictive dreaming can actually make you less, rather than more, anxious, because you know that your inner nocturnal radar will detect any true causes for concern in time for you to take evasive or positive action.

The real difference between free-floating worries and a true warning dream is that the latter tends to be very detailed, more urgent and have the quality of real life, but intensified, so that the immediacy remains with you all day.

People often describe such dreams as 'more than dreams', speaking of a golden light surrounding the scene.

A clear example is included in my book *Ghost Encounters*, describing how Jennifer's prophetic dream saved her mother's life. Jennifer's description was remarkably vivid, even down to details of the wallpaper in her daughter's bedroom and her late father's clothes:

In May, 1982, four months after my father died, I was asleep early in the morning. In my dreams, I heard a noise in my daughter Susan's room. Susan was staying with a girlfriend from school that weekend. I got up and went into my daughter's bedroom. My dad was standing by the wall. He was wearing a shiny grey suit in a silk-like material and there was a light all around his body. Just before his heart attack, my father had decorated my daughter's room in pink apple blossom so perhaps that is why he showed himself to me in that room.

My father's hands were warm to touch and he was well and glowing. 'Your mum's not well, so watch out,' he warned me and opened the door. I woke with a start next to my husband and woke him to tell him about my vivid dream. When my mother came, I asked her whether she was having any health problems. She denied this vehemently.

I mentioned the dream to my daughter Susan who was 14 and often stayed with my mother at weekends to keep her company. I asked her to keep an eye out for any problems. The next Sunday Susan came home and told me that when her grandmother had bent down, Susan had seen a red angry lump at the top of her breast which she had covered up quickly. I asked my mother about it and she said that she had not wanted to worry the family since my father had been ill. She had even kept her suspected illness from him.

I made my mother promise to go to the doctor at once. She was referred straight away to hospital. The lump was malignant, but after an operation and radiotherapy she recovered and had her 90th birthday in 1996.

Seeing Ghosts in Dreams

Many people who have lost relations in death have told me how immensely comforting dreams of them have proved. Sometimes the relation will hug the grieving person and talk of ordinary concerns that offer assurance that the deceased person is well and happy and essentially the same grandma or mother who fussed lovingly on earth. Whether such dreams are psychic contact from another dimension or our minds recreating the love that survives death matters less than the reassurance provided, especially if the death was sudden or came after a wasting illness.

Children routinely see deceased grandparents in dreams, and this can be a very positive way of coming to terms with the concept of death for the whole family. Such dreams are rarely frightening for the child.

Mary, who lives in County Wicklow in Ireland, described how her late husband came back to see his granddaughter in dreams:

When my granddaughter Marie was three years old, she told my daughter Sian that she had been talking to Grampy in a dream. She said that Grampy looked young, but said that there were no pubs in heaven and that his father was there too. Grandpa was wearing his pyjamas. On Grampy's next visit. Marie reported that he was wearing his shirt and trousers. Sian was pregnant and Grampy told Marie that Mummy would have the new baby very soon. He sent the message, 'You must not be disappointed that the baby is a girl again.'

Everybody was expecting a boy. It was Sian's third baby after two girls and the baby was a completely different shape in the womb. Sian had been calling him Shannon and buying blue things. Marie reported that Grandpa said the family could still call the girl Shannon, as it was a good Irish name. Soon after this conversation, Sian went into labour and the baby was a girl who was called Shannon.

Grampy did not visit Marie again until just before Sian's fourth baby was due. This time he assured Marie she was having a brother and that it would be coming straight away. The baby was born as predicted very shortly after Grandpa's visit, a boy called Connor.

The little girl identified her grandfather by describing his clothes and appearance, although she had never seen any photos of him and he had died when she was very tiny.

Children find it easier than adults to see deceased relatives because the demands of logic have not narrowed the bounds of possibility. If a grandfather loved a child in life and came to see him or her, for the young child death is no obstacle to continuing contact.

Dreaming of Loved Ones

Although such dream contact is normally quite spontaneous, you can recreate the closeness of a beloved mother, grandmother or partner. This can be especially helpful on anniversaries or when you are in early acute stages of grief.

You are not calling up spirits nor holding them back from moving on. From many distressing accounts I believe that seances, ouija boards and the like are dangerous on a psychological as well as a psychic level.

Psychic dreaming is simply a dimension in which love and comfort can be experienced with that easy and entirely positive acceptance children like Marie take for granted, that granny or granddad popped into a dream to have a chat.

☆ Choose an evening when you can be undisturbed and feel positive and pleasantly tired, rather than exhausted or fractious.

☆ Before you prepare yourself for sleep, light a small pink or green night light, the colours of family and love. Place it where it can burn away safely as you slumber.

☆ See yourself encircled with protective light (although those you love would never harm you).

☆ Play some gentle music that you and the person who has died shared as a special melody. As the songs unfold, hear again the familiar voice joining in with the words or humming the tune.

☆ Now add a fragrance that evokes for you the person's essence – a favourite perfume, lavender polish, newly baked bread, crisp linen.

☆ When the music is drawing to a close, hold a symbol of the person whom you have lost – a photograph, scarf, a much read book or a piece of jewellery. This artefact may have belonged to the deceased person. Equally it could be a gift that he or she gave you that was special, not in monetary terms, so much as offered and accepted in love.

☆ As you hold the focus of love and loss, recall in your mind's ear the voice of the person sharing a joke or a moment of intimacy.

☆ Visualise your loved one standing on the other side of the room. Concentrate on the patch of colour on his or her clothes, so that it gradually expands and builds up until you can see the person in your mind's eye.

☆ Blow out the candle and leave the object next to your bed or if it is small under your pillow.

☆ As you drift into sleep, hear the voice talking softly to you about everyday events.

☆ You may dream about the person in quite an ordinary context or the dream may bring to the surface any unresolved issues that may then be expressed symbolically and laid to rest. In the dream you may not see the figure clearly but just be aware of the presence.

☆ When you wake you will feel a great sense of peace, even if you cannot recall the specific dream.

☆ During the following days you may sense his or her presence, see a fleeting shadow or experience deep harmony. Some people detect the perfume of the loved one long after the physical scent has disappeared from the bedroom.

☆ After this you may experience other dreams of deceased

relations, perhaps even a figure you do not recognise.

☆ Delve into the family photographs or archives. You may identify a great-grandmother or grandfather offering them-self as a wise guide and who may thereafter return through dreams especially at times of crisis, bringing reassurance that all will be well and wise counsel. If this occurs you are very privileged. There is nothing to fear.

☆ If you do not welcome such contact, however, it will not continue. Family ghosts rarely intrude in dreams or actuality if their presence proves worrying, but you may still experi-ence a sense of being protected, especially as you drift into sleep.

☆ You can also use this technique to move closer emotion-ally to friends or family members who are still alive if you are estranged through misunderstanding or the person is temporarily absent because of physical distance.

☆ Again you may experience reconciliation in the dream and you may hear from them very soon or find a natural opportu-nity to make contact.

EXERCISE: KEEPING A DREAM JOURNAL

Use either a specially bound diary or one with loose leaf pages so that you can add and catalogue dreams. You can either use your initial notes along with any draw-ings, or copy them out in the journal as you play back a recording on tape.

☆ Date each entry, noting any significant events in your life at the time of the dream. This helps both when you come to analyse your dreams and in seeing what images recur so that you can trace the patterns.

☆ Give your dreams broad category titles, along with what seems to be a significant phrase or keyword, so that you can identify patterns between dreams and events. This forms a basis for eventually establishing your own dream symbol system.

☆ Note the location of each dream, its significance to you and the emotions it creates. If it is a place from the past, it may have special significance to your present situation, or be a rerun of an old situation needing resolution for you to move forward.

☆ Begin to record your own dream symbols, altering my list if my interpretations do not match your personal concepts. Many dream symbols are universal, but nevertheless how we perceive a meaning will depend on our own unique life path and the influences of culture and family upon our growing imagination as children.

EXERCISE: ENCOURAGING LUCID DREAMS

Many out-of-body experiences occur during lucid dreams, the state when you are aware that you are dreaming and so can control or even change the dream. Dream recall is the first important step towards lucid dreaming, which you can use to fly, float and travel to past times or other dimensions.

Once you are aware that the out-of-body experience is occurring in a dream and that therefore nothing physical can harm you, you can explore many scenarios that might be more daunting in more consciously induced astral projection from the waking state.

☆ Before you go to sleep, lie in bed and evoke in your mind an exciting dream in which you are flying, floating or exploring other dimensions. Concentrate on the colours, the details and the feelings of joy or anticipation.

☆ Focus on or create a dream symbol, something that would not occur in the everyday world, a talking animal, a rainbow flower that constantly changes colour or bright feathery wings emerging from your arms.

☆ When this sign appears repeat aloud: 'When I see [name your sign], I will recall that I am dreaming.'

☆ Continue with the visualisation, introducing the symbol several times, saying each time: 'When [name your sign] appears I will recall that I am dreaming and that I can change the action.'

☆ Let yourself fall asleep, but keep your intention to know you are dreaming and your dream symbol in your thoughts, so that these are the last remaining conscious words in your mind before falling asleep.

☆ When you wake, note in your psychic journal anything you can recall of your dreams and whether your special dream symbol occurred.

☆ It may help to have an actual symbol that you can hold while repeating the affirmation each night before sleep, such as a brightly coloured feather for your wings.

☆ Each morning just after you wake and each evening before sleep recreate your original visualised dream sequence, adding details, embellishing your symbol with even more elaborate detail and developing the picture.

9

Developing Your Psychic Work

Forms of Divination From the Natural World

Once you are confident in your own abilities, you can join a psychic organisation (see page 145 for some examples). For many people psychic awareness becomes, as it was for our ancestors, a skill that is mainly used in the everyday world to help with decision-making and to confirm the rightness of our feelings and actions. For example, you can scry, using the symbols listed at the end of this section as a guide to meaning, while walking, driving, washing clothes, having dinner by candlelight or lying in the bath. The methods listed below span all times and cultures.

Divination With Clouds

Cloud divination, which was practised by the Druids, involves scrying by watching the changing shapes of the clouds, letting them stimulate your natural abilities. As a cloud shape may shift two or three times as you watch it, this can build a series of images that will answer your question or current dilemma, much as a Tarot spread builds up a picture.

☆ Concentrate on one area in the sky. Look for large single dark clouds against clear blue sky or a dense cumulus cloud formation at sunrise or sunset.

☆ Once you have identified two or three images, scribble sketches of them on paper. Let your intuition put them together in its own time.

Divination With Fire

☆ Light a bonfire in the garden or a small open fire in a grate.

☆ Write a question or dilemma on a piece of paper, cast it into the flame. As it flares up and dies down, look in the fire around the ashes for pictures or impressions that may offer an answer.

Divination With Herbs

Use dried or finely chopped fresh herbs. The traditional divinatory herbs are parsley, sage, rosemary and thyme, but any culinary herbs are suitable as long as the individual leaves are solid and separate rather than powdery.

☆ Place the herbs in a shallow glass or ceramic dish. Take out a handful.

☆ Holding the paper taut at either end, shake the herbs onto a piece of stiff white kitchen paper or card with a rough surface until an image is formed.

☆ Herb pictures can often be whole scenes, viewed from a distance.

☆ If your herb picture does not make sense immediately, sit at the other side of the table to change your viewpoint.

Divination With Tea Leaves

We can all read the tea leaves, just like our grandmothers. The secret lies in letting a group of leaves suggest an image or picture that may shed light on present matters and future options.

☆ Make a pot of tea using a traditional brew such as Earl Grey or Darjeeling. Do not use a strainer when you pour out your tea.

☆ Use a large, plain, light-coloured cup.

☆ When you have drunk the tea, leave sufficient liquid in the bottom of the cup so that the tea leaves are still floating.

☆ Swirl the remaining tea round in the cup in an anti-clockwise direction three times with the left hand.

☆ Place the inverted cup in the saucer to drain the remaining liquid. Turn the inverted cup a further three times in an anti-clockwise direction, once again using the left hand.

☆ Keeping the handle towards you, turn the cup the right way up and twist it in all directions until you can see images in the leaves.

Divination With Soap Suds and Bubbles

☆ Handwash an item that needs scrubbing using soap so that it makes bubbles on the surface of the water.

☆ Let the suds form pictures and see what associations flow consciously from your subconscious mind.

☆ Alternatively, run a bath and add a foaming oil. As you lie in it, move the bubbles with your fingers to make pictures. If you use a lavender or jasmine fragrance, the aroma will enhance your natural psychic powers.

Divination With Molten Wax

☆ Light a brightly coloured candle.

☆ Fill a heatproof pottery or metal bowl with cold water.

☆ Think of a question or dominating concern as you gaze into the candle flame.

☆ Tip a single candle drop by drop on the surface of the water, thinking of a question or issue that concerns you.

☆ Allow the wax to set into an image. Concentrate on this image and what it means to you.

Core Symbols

The following dream and scrying symbols are mainly archetypal images that have had relevance in different periods, cultures and mythologies. They can be used for any kind of psychic interpretation, although the geometric shapes are most usually seen in water, herb or tea-leaf scrying and falling and floating images are associated with dreams.

It may be that a symbol has either a positive or negative aspect for you. Let your feelings guide you. Is the forest in the teacup or mirror an exciting one or are you lost and frightened? Each symbol has two sides, positive and *negative (indicated in italics)*. Only you can decide which aspect applies to your particular circumstances.

Collect your own symbols to add to the list.

Alien, Strange Creature: The need to follow your own path. *A feeling of being isolated and misunderstood.*

Angels: Seek happiness through psychic and spiritual development, ideals, wisdom and connection with your higher self or spirit guides. *Being out of touch with practical issues.*

Anchor: Material security and emotional stability. *Drifting off course.*

Ants, Insects: Joining with others will overcome a seemingly immovable situation. *Annoyance or being overwhelmed by petty irritations.*

Apple: Fertility and abundance; efforts will bear fruit. *Unless an idea or relationship is nurtured, it will not thrive.*

Bat: Trust your instincts. Hidden fears of the unknown will melt if faced in the light of day. *Someone is keeping a secret from you.*

Bees: Positive communication with others and with your evolving psychic self, helpful mother figures. *Misunderstandings in communication.*

Bells: A cause to rejoice, especially associated with weddings and relationships. *Let others know of your efforts.*

Birds: Messages, soaring ambitions; family members spreading their wings. *Caged birds indicate fears of being trapped.*

Boats, Ferries: Travel, positive changes, expansion of horizons, results from past efforts. *Sinking ships represent uncertainty about impending changes.*

Book: An open book represents a new opportunity through learning or in legal matters. *A closed book says there are secrets you need to know.*

Bull: A very ancient symbol of power, courage and determination, tackling problems head on. *Fears about potentially uncontrollable irritability and anger in self or others.*

Butterfly: Rebirth and regeneration, enjoy present happiness. *A trapped or dying butterfly indicates the time to let go.*

Bridge: There is a way to overcome present difficulties if you look hard enough. Meet people halfway to resolve conflicts. *A broken bridge can represent the weak link in a plan or relationship.*

Castle, Palace: Success and recognition, protection of a powerful force or person. *Feelings of exclusion if outside or trapped inside* (see also **Prison**).

Cats Independence, an untamed spirit – a very positive self-image. *Fierce or black witches' cats can represent hidden spite in others or one's own resentful feelings.*

Children, Babies: New projects; if a parent or prospective parent, joy through children. *An excessive desire to return to the past, insecurity and a desire to be protected.*

Circle or Ring, Circles: A relationship or partnership will become more permanent, the successful completion of a project. *Going round in circles.*

Crabs: Present illness or problems will end; the emergence of new confidence. *A crab scuttling under rocks indicates an inability to show feelings.*

Crocodile: Stealth, outward calm and patience will bring results. *Beware of double-dealing in a friendly stranger or new acquaintance.*

Cross: Limitations and obstacles to be overcome. *A*

personal sacrifice is necessary — but the short-term pain will bring long-term gain.

Dagger, Knife: Cut through inertia; use logic rather than emotion. *Fears of hostility, unwarranted gossip and malice.*

Dashes: Enterprises and gains that will take time to mature. *Carelessness over detail.*

Dogs: Fidelity and loyal friendship. *Ferocious dogs indicate suppressed anger and aggression.*

Door: If ajar, a new opening to be taken. *If closed, an avenue that is not yet open.*

Dots: Money or money-making opportunities. *Worrying about perfection.*

Dove: Act as a peacemaker between warring family or close friends. *You may risk being coerced into an unwise decision to keep the peace.*

Dragons   Power, energy and assured success. *Destructive urges or sexual frustration.*

Ear: A time for listening, not talking, hear what people mean rather than what they say. *Gossip about those close to you.*

Eclipse: One aspect of life will temporarily dominate. *Being temporarily overshadowed by others or the needs of others.*

Egg: Fertility; new beginnings. *A fragile ego or vulnerable person must be nurtured.*

Elephant: Wise counsel; a long-term worthwhile undertaking. *Seemingly immovable obstacles.*

Falling, Figure Falling Through Air: Letting go of inhibitions, opening the self to new experience. *Fear of losing security, of letting go of control.*

Fighting, Armies, Soldiers: Taking action against injustice, courage and action. *A long, entrenched struggle.*

Fire: Illumination and renewal of energies; clearing out what is no longer needed. *An unresolved conflict that periodically flares up.*

Fish, Fisherman: Future prosperity; success through patience. *Being manipulated by others.*

Floating: Sexual harmony, connection with your own unconscious wisdom and the deeper wisdom of mankind. *A sense of isolation and aimlessness.*

Flying, Parachutes, Planes, Non-angelic Beings With Wings: Astral travel, sexual ecstasy; new opportunities, taking control of destiny. *Fears of losing control emotionally or sexuality.*

Forest, Jungle: Trusting your instincts; a potentially exciting, unexpected direction. *A sense of having lost the way; being unable to see the way forward because of numerous pressures.*

Fox: Adaptability, the need for stealth and ingenuity. *Potential treachery by others.*

Giant: A great ambition or undertaking; help from powerful sources. *Intimidating people who should not be allowed to dominate.*

Gift: An unexpected bonus or accolade is coming your way. *Be aware that an offer comes with a price which may or may not be worth paying.*

Gnome, Dwarf: Resolution of financial problems; practical advice that should be heeded. *Buried hopes and dreams or repressed instincts.*

Grandmother, Wise Woman, Witch: Wisdom and protection, learning from past experience. *Fears about ageing and ugliness; unresolved or unacknowledged conflict with an older woman.*

Gypsy: Desire to be free of unnecessary restrictions, emerging psychic abilities. *Restlessness; a feeling of alienation, especially in a domestic situation.*

Head: Use logic rather than feelings to guide your decisions. *Too cold and logical a approach to a situation or relationship.*

Heart: Follow your heart whether in love or family matters. *Emotional blackmail by others.*

Hills, Mountains: Long-term aims and dreams that are within reach. *Slow progress, obstacles, a sense of a constant uphill struggle.*

Horse: Harmony with others; expanding horizons and opportunities. *Being carried along a path you do not wish to follow.*

Key: The answer to a long-standing problem. *Locked emotions, delays of all kinds.*

Knot: Concentrate all your energies on one area; focus priorities. *A tangle of emotions or practical problems from which you feel you cannot free yourself.*

Iceberg: Hidden depths to a person or situation. *Ignoring the deeper implications of an action.*

Island: Holidays, the need to rest and relax. *Feelings of isolation.*

Juggler: Successfully balancing different demands. *Being asked to meet conflicting demands.*

Ladder: Ambitions, ideals and dreams that can be achieved step by step. *Fears of aiming high and failing.*

Leaves: A cluster of leaves indicates praise or material rewards. *A single falling leaf warns that something is dying and that it is time to move on.*

Light, Lighthouse: Enlightenment, spiritual and psychic dreams; the transition to deeper awareness. *Being attracted by superficial qualities in others.*

Lines (straight):   A direct course, a straightforward journey or enterprise. *Too rigid an attitude to problems and people.*

Lines (wavy or broken):   The need to take detours to achieve an aim. *Frustration, especially in travel.*

Lions, Tigers, Wild Animals: Instinctive survival energies; strength and courage; awakening sexuality. *Representing negative feelings, anger and sexuality.*

Loop: Finding an alternative approach if the way ahead is blocked. *Pointless disagreements; impulsive decisions that could be unwise.*

Magician: Creative power, inspiration and all matters psychic. *Beware illusion and taking the easy path; avoid offers that seem too good to be true.*

Mask: Presenting the right persona to the world; using tact, creativity and imagination. *Being uncertain of the intentions and responses of others; revealed secrets.*

Maze: The exploration and revelation of hidden wisdom; finding the way out of a difficult situation. *Confusion about future plans and direction, perhaps because others have been giving conflicting messages.*

Meteor, Comet: Sudden illumination; seize the moment, a sudden opportunity may not come again. *The temptation to seek excitement rather than reliability.*

Monk, Nun, Priest, Hermit: Wise counsel, from an older person or established source, on matters of the heart and spirit. *An inability by an older person to relate to the real feelings and needs of others.*

Monkey: Curiosity, adaptability and the acquisition of new skills. *Deviousness and vacillation in others.*

Moon: Following rather than resisting natural cycles and stages of life, trusting intuition and dreams. *Illusion and deception; unrealistic expectations; inaction.*

Musical Notes: Harmony with self and others. *People close to you are causing trouble among family or friends.*

Necklace: A bond of friendship or love encircles you. *A broken necklace suggests that friendship or love needs attention.*

Octopus: Versatility; the ability to meet different demands simultaneously. *Inability to disentangle from an* *emotional situation, possessiveness in others.*

Owl: Considered thought; wise counsel on worldly matters. *Inadvisability of ignoring warnings from an older or wiser person.*

Parrot: Be original; suggest and implement new ideas, rather than following established approaches. *Gossip and chatter may prove irritating.*

Pipe: Take time to think over and discuss a major decision. *Avoid the smokescreen cast by others over facts or feelings.*

Prison, Cage: Recognising that certain instinctive reactions and words need to be temporarily restrained. *Feelings of being stifled and unable to speak or act freely.*

Pyramid: Healing, psychic powers; a need to look to the past for the answer. *Storing up resources when it might be wiser to use them.*

Rainbow: New beginnings, joy after sorrow; future prosperity. *Disappointment; unrealistic dreams.*

Rats, Mice, Rodents: Success of persistence to overcome inertia and stagnation. *Issues that seem to multiply by the day, but cannot be ignored.*

Rectangle: Progress by accepting constraints following a set path. *Rigid attitudes by others may reduce the scope for immediate action.*

Rocks: Using setbacks as an impetus to make even greater progress. *Potential hazards to be negotiated with care.*

Roses, Flowers: Love, friendship and emotional happiness; bouquets are expressions of love or admiration. *Dying flowers indicate hidden disharmony or health worries.*

Scales: Justice and principles are important right now. Balance the pros and cons of a situation carefully. *Danger of being swayed by emotion or prejudice.*

Signs, Signposts: Choices in future paths, follow the indicators of likely success. *Confusion lies ahead; conflicting choices.*

Snake: Regeneration; shedding past troubles. *Others may be less than open in their dealings.*

Square: Protection, a time of preparation; material security. *Preoccupation with financial and practical matters restricts scope for change.*

Stalks, Sticks: People who will feature prominently in your life. Two or three are a family; a large group can represent an organisation. Straight stalks indicate reliability. *Wavy or broken stalks represent those who vary their opinions according to mood and situation.*

Stars: Dreams that can be realised; the evolving psychic senses. *Waiting for others to fulfil happiness.*

Sun: A universal symbol of joy, the life force, expansion, confidence and communication. *Physical or emotional exhaustion; lack of relief from intense pressures.*

Table: Family togetherness and celebrations. *Hold a family or work conference to resolve potential misunderstandings.*

Telescope: Look for the long-term advantage rather than immediate gain or relief. *Problems may be magnified by anxiety.*

Thorns: A developing relationship or area of life that needs gentleness and protection from the interference of others. *Small but painful barbs inflicted by others.*

Tower: Take a necessary stand on principle, a wider viewpoint will emerge. *Feeling bound by restrictions not of your making.*

Treasure Chest: An undeveloped talent or new contact will bring you financial benefit. *Drains on your financial resources.*

Triangle: Unexpected possibilities or undeveloped talents that can lead to success. *Opportunities must be seized before they are missed.*

Visitors: News or information especially from abroad; the renewal of old friendships or ties. *Intrusion into your privacy or home life.*

Volcano: A sudden upsurge of powerful inner energy or deep-seated change that will shake the inertia of those around. *Repressed anger or resentment that may burst forth in a destructive way if not channelled.*

Well: Health, healing abilities and access to unconscious wisdom through psychic exploration. *Loss of vitality and optimism.*

Wolf: The family; nurturing others; loyalty. *Feeling torn apart by family or work conflicts.*

Web: The coming together of different aspects of life in a pattern, creating your future by present actions. *Feeling trapped by fate and the machinations of others.*

Useful Addresses

Aromatherapy

United Kingdom

Courses and Details of Practitioners:
The International Society of Professional Aromatherapists, Hinckley and District Hospital and Health Centre (Head Office), The Annexe, Mount Road, Hinckley, Leics. LE10 1AG. Tel: 01455 637987.
They accredit all courses and training.

Oils by Mail Order:
Neals Yard Remedies, 15 Neal's Yard, London WC2H 9DP. Tel: 0171-379 0141.
Kobashi Essential Oils, 2 Fore Street, Ide, Exeter, Devon EX2 9RQ. Tel: 01392 217628. Fax: 01392 427090.
Tisserand, Aromatherapy Products Ltd, Newtown Road, Hove, Sussex BN3 7BA. Tel: 01273 325666.
Fax 01273 208444.

United States

National Holistic Aromatherapy Association, PO Box 18622, Boulder, CO 803-0622. Tel: (303) 258 2791.

Crystals

Australia

The Mystic Trader, 125 Flinders Lane, Melbourne 3000. Tel: 03 650 4477.
Mail order as well as personal service.

South Africa

The Wellstead, 1 Wellington Avenue, Wynberg, Cape 7300. Tel: 797 8982.
Mail order.
Topstone Mining Corporation CC, Dido Valley Road, PO Box 20, Simonstown 7975. Tel: (0121) 86-2020/1/2/3.

United Kingdom

The Mystic Trader, 60 Chalk Farm Road, London NW1 8AN. Tel: 0171-284 0141.
Mysteries, 7 Monmouth Street, London WC2H 9DA. Tel: 0171-240 3688.
Shop and mail order, everything for the New Age, plus good advice.

United States

Eye of the Cat, 3314 E. Broadway, Long Beach, CA 90803. Tel: (213) 438 3569.
Mail order crystals and other New Age commodities.
The Crystal Cave, 415 West Foothill Blvd, Claremont, CA 91711.
Mail order. Stocks a huge variety of crystal and stones.

Dreams

United Kingdom

Institute for Psychophysical Research, Celia Green, 118 Banbury Road, Oxford OX2 6JU.
Lucid dreams.
Confederation of Healing Organisations, 113 High Street, Berkhamstead, Herts HP4 2DJ. Tel: 01442 870667.
Dream therapy.

United States

Association for the Study of Dreams, PO Box 1600, Vienna, VA 22183.
Lucidity Institute, 2555 Park Blvd #2, Palo Alto, CA 94306-1919. Email: faq@lucidity.com.
For research, information on lucid dreaming.

Herbs

Australia

The National Herbalists Association of Australia, PO Box 65, Kingsgrove, NSW 2208.
Professional organisation.

United Kingdom

The National Institute of Medical Herbalists, 56 Longbrook Street, Exeter, Devon EX4 6AH.
Professional organisation.
The Herb Society, PO Box 599, London SW11 4BW.
Information on herbs.

Suppliers

G Baldwin and Co., 171–3 Walworth Road, London SE17 1RW. Tel: 0171-703 5550.
Largest range of herbs and herbal products in the UK, extensive mail order.
Island Herbs, Vicki and Ian Foss, Sunacre, The Terrace, Chale, Ventnor, Isle of Wight PO38 2HL. Tel: 01983 730288.
Wide variety of culinary and medicinal herbs for garden and window box. All plants grown on site. Send SAE for list.
Gerard House, 736 Christchurch Road, Bournemouth BH7 6BZ. Tel: 01202 434116.
Good for dried mail-order herbs.

United States

The American Herbalists Guild, PO Box 1683, Soquel, CA 95073.
Professional organisation.

Suppliers

Joan Teresa Power Products, PO Box 442, Mars Hill, NC 28754. Tel: (704) 689 5739.
Mail order, especially for unusual herbs, plants, oils and incenses.
The Sage Garden, PO Box 144, Payette, ID 83661.
Tel: (208) 454 2026.
Mail order, for herbs, also oils, amulets and incenses.

Meditation

See also New Age Music.

United Kingdom

Organisations

The School of Meditation, 158 Holland Park Avenue, London W11 4UH. Tel: 0171-603 6116.

Meditation and Visualisation Music

Beechwood Music, Littleton House, Littleton Road, Ashford, Middlesex TW15 1UU.

United States

Meditation and Visualisation Music

Raven Recordings, 744 Broad Street, Room 1815, Newark, NJ 07102. Tel: (201) 642 7942.

Meditation music, videos and tapes by Gabrielle Roth, an expert on the subject.

Mediumship and Spiritualism

Australia

Australian Spiritualist Association, PO Box 248, Canterbury, NSW 2193.

Canberra Spiritualist Association, Griffin Centre, Civic, Canberra.

Canada

Spiritualist Church of Canada, 1835 Lawrence Avenue East, Scarborough, Ontario M1R 2Y3.

Walter J. Meyer zu Erpen, Survival Research Institute of Canada, PO Box 8697, Victoria, British Columbia V8W 3S3.
E-mail: gateway@nucleus.com — *The Directory of Spiritualist Organizations in Canada* is published by the Survival Research Institute of Canada. A copy can be obtained by sending your details and 5 Canadian dollars to the above address.

United Kingdom

Spiritualist Association of Great Britain, 33 Belgrave Square, London SW1 8QL. Tel: 0171-235 3351.
The Arthur Findlay College, Stanstead Hall, Stanstead, Mountfitchet, Essex CM24 8UD.
This is also the address of the Spiritualist National Union.

New Age Music

Australia

New World Productions, PO Box 244 WBO, Red Hill, Queensland 4059. Tel: 007 33667 0788.
Mail order.

United Kingdom

New World Cassettes, Freepost, Paradise Farm, Westhall, Halesworth, Suffolk IP19.
Free mail order catalogue.

Paganism

The Pagan Federation, BM Box 7097, London WC1N 3XX.
An umbrella organisation for pagan and wiccan contacts in the UK with links to international pagan organisations.

Parapsychology, Psychic Study Societies and Colleges

Ireland

Irish UFO/Paranormal Research Association, Box 3070, Whitehall, Dublin 9.

United Kingdom

ASSAP (Association for the Scientific Study of Anomalous Phenomena), Dr Hugh Pincott, St Aldhelm, 20 Paul Street, Frome, Somerset BA11 1DX. Tel: 01373 451777.

Fountain International, 35 Padacre Road, Torquay, Devon TQ2 8PX.

An organisation that hopes to improve the world through meditation, crystals and spiritual awareness.

The Ghost Club, Tom Perrott, 93 The Avenue, Muswell Hill, London N10 2QG. Tel: 0181-883 1091.

Haunted Scotland, 35 South Dean Road, Kilmarnock, Ayrshire KA3 7RD. Tel: 01563 539509.

A bi-monthly magazine produced by Mark and Hannah Fraser who will also help with any ghost sightings or problems with hauntings. They are always glad to receive accounts from anywhere in the world, but especially Scotland.

The Churches Fellowship for Spiritual and Psychic Studies, The Rural Workshop, South Road, North Somercotes, Louth, Lincolnshire LN11 7BT.

The College of Psychic Studies, 16 Queensberry Place, London SW7 2EB

The Scottish Society for Psychical Research, Secretary and Newsletter Editor, Daphne Plowman, 131 Stirling Drive, Bishopbriggs, Glasgow G64 3AX. Tel: 0141 772 4588.

United States

American Society for Psychical Research, 5 West 73rd Street, New York, NY 10023.

Ghost Trackers Journal, PO Box 205, Oaklawn, IL 60454.

Parapsychology Foundation Counselling Bureau, 228 E 7st Street, New York, NY 10021.

Strange, PO Box 2246, Rockville, MD 20852.

Paranormal research organisation.

Shamanism

United Kingdom

Eagle's Wing Centre for Contemporary Shamanism, BCM Box 7475, London WC1N 3XX.
Faculty of Shamanics, Kenneth and Beryl Meadows,
PO Box 300, Potters Bar, Hertfordshire EN6 4LE.

United States

Dance of the Deer Foundation, Center for Shamanic Studies, PO Box 699, Soquel, CA 95073. Tel: (408) 475-9560. Fax: (408) 475-1860. Email: shaman@shamanism.com.

Spiritual Healing

Canada

National Federation of Spiritual Healers (Canada), call for information (416) 284 4798.

United Kingdom

British Alliance of Healing Associations, Jo Wallace, 3 Sandy Lane, Gisleham, Lowestoft, Suffolk NR33 8EQ.
Tel: 01502 742224.
National Federation of Spiritual Healers, Old Manor Farm Studio, Church Street, Sunbury-on-Thames, Middlesex TW16 6RG. Tel: 01932 783164.

United States

World of Light, PO Box 425, Wappingers Falls, NY 12590. Phone/Fax: (914) 297 2867.

Further Reading

Aromatherapy and Incenses

Cunningham, Scott, *The Complete Book of Oils, Incense and Brews*, Llewellyn, 1993

Price, Shirley, *Practical Aromatherapy*, Thorsons, 1996

Tisserand, Maggie, *Aromatherapy for Women*, Thorsons, 1995

Tisserand, Robert, *Aromatherapy for Everyone*, Penguin, 1990

Worword, Valerie Ann, *The Fragrant Pharmacy*, Bantam, 1996

Auras and Chakras

Andrews, Ted, *How to See and Read the Aura*, Llewellyn, 1994

Brennan, Barbara Ann, *Hands of Light, A Guide to Healing Through the Human Energy Field*, Bantam, 1987

Ozaniec, Naomi, *The Elements of the Chakras*, Element, 1989

Candles

Buckland, Ray, *Advanced Candle Magick*, Llewellyn, 1997

Buckland, Ray, *Practical Candleburning Rituals*, Llewellyn, 1982

Crystals

Cunningham, Scott, *Encyclopaedia of Crystal, Gem and Metal Magic*, Llewllyn, 1991

Holbeche, Soozi, *The Power of Gems and Crystals*, Piatkus, 1989

Divination

Eason, Cassandra, *The Complete Guide to Divination*, Piaktus, 1998

Dreams

Laberge, Stephen and Rheingold, Howard, *Exploring the World of Lucid Dreaming*, Ballantine, 1990

Lewis, James R., *The Dream Encyclopaedia*, Visible Ink, 1995

Parker, Derek and Julia, *The Secret World of Your Dreams*, Piatkus, 1996

General Mind, Body, Spirit

Button, John, and Bloom, William, *The Seeker's Guide, a New Age Resource Book*, Thorsons, 1992

Evans, Hilary, *Frontiers of Reality: Where Science Meets the Paranormal*, Thorsons, 1989

Guiley, Rosemary Ellen, *Encyclopaedia of Mystical and Paranormal Experience*, Diamond Books, 1993

Randles, Jenny, *The Paranormal Source Book*, Piatkus, 1996

Wilson, Colin, *The Giant Book of the Supernatural*, Parragon, 1995

Ghosts and Exploring the Past

Eason Cassandra, *Discover Your Past Lives*, Quantum, 1996

Eason, Cassandra, *Encountering Ghosts*, Blandford, 1997

Prince Michael of Greece, *Living with Ghosts*, Norton, 1995

Spencer, John and Anne, *The Encyclopaedia of Ghosts and Spirits*, Headline, 1992

Williamson, Linda, *Contacting the Spirit World*, Piatkus, 1996
Wilson, Colin, *The Atlas of Holy Places and Sacred Sites*, Dorling Kindersley, 1996

Herbalism

Culpeper, Nicholas, *Culpeper's Colour Herbal*, Foulsham, 1983
Cunningham, Scott, *Encyclopaedia of Herbs*, Llewllyn, 1997

Meditation and Visualisation

Brown, Barbara, *New Mind, New Body,* Bantam, 1975
Graham, Helen, *Visualisation: An Introductory Guide*, Piatkus, 1996
LeShan, Lawrence, *How to Meditate*, Crucible, 1989

Shamanism

Casteneda, Carlos, *Journey to Ixtlan*, Penguin, 1972
Vittebsky, Piers, *The Shaman*, Macmillan, 1995
Walsh, Roger N., *The Spirit of Shamanism*, Tarcher, 1990

Telepathy, Premonitions, Psychic Development

Cooper, Joe, *The Mystery of Telepathy*, Constable, 1982
Eason, Cassandra, *The Complete Guide to Psychic Development*, Piatkus, 1997
Eysenck, Hans L. and Sargent, Karl, *Explaining the Unexplained*, Weidenfield and Nicolson, 1982

Index